THE
FOUNDING
FATHERS ON
LEADERSHIP

ALSO BY DONALD T. PHILLIPS

Lincoln on Leadership: Executive Strategies for Tough Times
On the Brink: The Life and Leadership of Norman Brinker
(with Norman Brinker)
Lincoln Stories for Leaders

THE FOUNDING FATHERS ON LEADERSHIP

CLASSIC TEAMWORK IN CHANGING TIMES

DONALD T. PHILLIPS

WARNER BOOKS

A Time Warner Company

Warner Books, Inc., 1271 Avenue of the Americas, New York, NY 10020
Visit our Web site at http://warnerbooks.com

 A Time Warner Company

Printed in the United States of America
First Printing: November 1997
10 9 8 7 6 5 4 3 2 1

Library of Congress Cataloging-in-Publication Data

Phillips, Donald T. (Donald Thomas)
    The founding fathers on leadership : classic teamwork in changing
time / Donald T. Phillips.
        p. cm.
    Includes bibliographical references.
    ISBN 0-446-52092-6
    1. United States—Politics and government—1775–1783.
    2. Political leadership—United States—History—18th century.
    3. Industrial management.   4. Organizational effectiveness—United
States—Case studies.   5. Statesmen—United States—History—18th
century.   I. Title.
E210.P53   1997
303.3'4'097309033—DC21   97-7014
                                                              CIP

Book design by Giorgetta Bell McRee

Contents

"Wise statesmen as they were, they knew the tendency of prosperity to breed tyrants, and so they established these great self-evident truths, that when in the distant future some man, some faction, some interest, should set up the doctrine that none but rich men, or none but white men, were entitled to life, liberty and the pursuit of happiness, their posterity might look up again to the Declaration of Independence . . . so that truth, and justice, and mercy, and all the humane and Christian virtues might not be extinguished from the land."

Abraham Lincoln,
on the founding fathers,
August 17, 1858

Introduction

It was a time of great change. A time when one thing was on the way out and another on the way in.

Old and current value systems were being challenged. For centuries, people the world over had been oppressed through tyrannical monarchies and dictatorships. There were no forms of government on earth that guaranteed, or even advocated rights for the individual—let alone freedom itself.

There was anxiety among the masses, with much dissent and dissatisfaction. There was fear of the unknown—and yet a strong desire for something better. On one hand, people wanted change. On the other, they resisted it when it hit too close to home. There was comfort in the old ways.

Dissent soon turned to action by way of passionate civil disobedience. And, finally, civil disobedience itself metamorphosed into full-scale revolution.

But the period surrounding the American Revolution was also a time of tremendous creativity and innovation. There were no precedents for what was about to happen.

Clearly, something was waiting to be born.

The spark of a fire that would eventually burn around the world began in the so-called New World—in the thirteen American colonies, most of which were formed in the seventeenth century by people seeking a better life than they had experienced in Europe. By the mid-eighteenth century, all the colonies had become members of the British empire. Due to geographic location, along with the wisdom of old King George II, Americans were pretty much allowed to run their own affairs.

Philadelphia, with a population of 34,000, was the largest city in America and second largest in the overseas British empire. New York had a population of 22,000 in the north and, in the south, Charleston, with approximately 10,000 people, was the chief port of economic activity. Because Americans were prolific producers of goods, they had a dynamic and prosperous economy. As a matter of fact, America was famous for its "ragged currency"—so named because it changed hands frequently.

American autonomy, however, was significantly disrupted when, at the age of twenty-two, George III ascended to the throne of Great Britain in 1760. Not as wise or benevolent as his grandfather, the new King immediately set out to establish his power and influence over the Americans. His mental attitude and initial actions were like those of a modern tyrannical boss who arrives to run a new organization—with no respect for the culture or individuals that are already in place. Worse yet, the youthful George III attempted to impose his will and personal values on a proud and fiercely independent people.

One of the empire's first moves against the colonies was to establish the Revenue Act of 1764 (better known as the Sugar Act), which imposed a duty on American imports of molasses as well as limiting distribution from the West Indies to America. The effect on American production of distilled whiskey and rum was devastating. Massachusetts, Rhode Island, New York, and Pennsylvania immediately united and sent out numerous protestations to London—all of which fell on deaf ears. While Americans never did like being told what to do—and usually ignored previous edicts or orders—Great

Britain was now threatening their very livelihood. And that was a different matter altogether.

On August 14, 1764, an effigy was hung from an elm tree in Boston's Hanover Square. Beside it was a large black boot with a devil crawling out of the opening (symbolizing the Earl of Bute, an unpopular British official). The "Liberty Tree," as it soon came to be known, became a gathering point for dissident, sometimes riotous Americans. And beating the effigy or the boot was symbolic of striking a blow for freedom.

As tempers and passions began to rise, the American people became something of a volcano waiting to erupt. Just one major quake was necessary to set them off. And Great Britain provided that catalyst with imposition of a series of new oppressive government decrees.

The Quartering Act of 1765, for example, permitted the quartering of British troops in private residences without the permission of homeowners (which gave a hint of future British plans). But it was the Stamp Act of that same year that really caused a major crisis. The creation of this new tax (requiring stamps purchased from the British government be placed on nearly all publicly sold documents) incited immediate and spontaneous riots across the colonies. Poor people were thrown out of work because their employers could not afford to pay both them *and* the government. As a result, British officials were seized and beaten by American citizens and the slogan "No taxation without representation" was heard all across the land.

Great Britain was equally defiant toward the American upstarts. After repealing the Stamp Act in 1766, the government added the Declaratory Act, which proclaimed Parliament's supreme power over the colonies in both legislation and taxation. And then, in 1767, the royal government implemented the Townshend Acts—a series of external taxes levied on imports from England. More important, however, was the fact that these new decrees subtly provided for all economic controls to pass from local government authority to handpicked representatives of the British Crown. Unauthorized warrants and seizures were now sanctioned and, with time, American fiscal affairs were to be controlled by Great Britain.

At first the Townshend Acts did not create a great deal of reaction. And, certainly, there was no organized revolutionary movement in America. Gradually and steadily, however, a determination to resist British authority grew among businessmen, merchants, skilled professionals, and astute southern plantation owners.

In April 1768, after John Hancock defiantly prevented an inspection of one of his cargo ships, the British government filed criminal charges against him. This was not an act that went unnoticed, because Hancock was one of Boston's wealthiest and most influential businessmen. Even though the charges were eventually dropped, individual disobedience of British law became more and more common.

On October 1, 1768, a large number of British troops landed in Boston to quell the dissidents and provide coercive support for the local officials. But residents of Boston deeply resented the presence of troops and, almost immediately, groups of radicals began roaming the streets of Boston picking fights with soldiers.

Finally on March 5, 1770, the British opened fire on one band of unarmed citizens—killing five and wounding six. Word quickly spread throughout the colonies of "The Boston Massacre," and public outrage began to reach a crescendo. In spontaneous and unrelated events, Liberty Trees were consecrated from South Carolina to Connecticut as Americans rallied against the tyranny of England.

After a few years of feeble attempts to quell the outrage, Great Britain finally repealed the Townshend Acts. But only a few months later, in March 1773, the Crown (through the newly formed Gaspee Commission) took the unprecedented step of assuming power to negate trial by jury in the American colonies. And then, in an effort to rescue the near-bankrupt East India Company, Parliament passed the Tea Act of 1773. Already alarmed at the threat of a British monopoly on tea, Americans were further outraged when Tory merchants (British businessmen in America) were granted sole rights to sell the tea.

In protest, a group of Bostonians, thinly disguised as Indians, headed for Griffin's Wharf late on the evening of December 16, 1773. There, in what has since become known as the "Boston Tea Party," they boarded ships from the British East India Company and threw 342 chests of tea overboard into Boston Harbor.

When news of this latest defiant act reached England, the government reacted angrily. On January 29, 1774, the British Privy Council summoned Benjamin Franklin, who was in London as an agent for the Massachusetts state legislature. At that meeting the solicitor general, Alexander Wedderburn, spent more than an hour dressing down Franklin and assailing his virtue and character. All the sixty-eight-year-old American could do was to stand there in silence—and take it.

The British Parliament then passed the Boston Port Bill, which created a blockade of Boston Harbor—closing off all overseas trade and coastal shipping until the East India Company was repaid for its lost tea. Parliament also passed several more measures that, combined with the other acts of oppression, were quickly labeled the "Intolerable Acts." These included the Massachusetts Government Act (which dissolved the local government, abolished town meetings, and prevented the passage of new legislation), the Impartial Administration of Justice Act (in which those accused of capital crimes were sent to England for trial and punishment), and the Quebec Act (which seized colonial lands by extending the boundaries of British Canadian territory to the Ohio and Mississippi rivers).

By September 1774, Boston was, in effect, under siege. Its

citizens were starving; as businesses were closed down, hundreds of people were thrown out of work; personal property values fell drastically; thousands fled to nearby towns and villages. When November rolled around, about a dozen British regiments were occupying the city. And General Thomas Gage, acting governor of Massachusetts (who authorized the use of force to maintain authority), had only contempt for the local citizenry—referring to them as "a rude rabble . . . without plan, concert, or conduct." "What fools you are," he told American leaders, "to pretend to resist the power of Great Britain."

The siege of Boston, coupled with the Intolerable Acts, raised the conflict between Great Britain and the American colonies to a new level. As word spread, food and supplies began arriving in Boston from Philadelphia, Baltimore, Windham (Connecticut), Kingston (New Hampshire), and Essex County (Virginia). And soon all the other colonies rallied to the aid of their neighbors in Massachusetts. The American people were absolutely outraged by the incursions and oppressive acts taken by the British Crown. One wagonload of food was accompanied with a note of support: "Consider we are all embarked in [the same boat] and must sink or swim together."

In Massachusetts, citizens became committed and stood ready to preserve their homeland. "Death is more [acceptable] than slavery," resolved a group in Marlborough. "A free-born people are not required to submit to tyranny."

When General Gage sent troops to seize a supply of gunpowder in nearby Charlestown, frantic rumors began to spread that the British were on a rampage of pillage and torture. In less than twenty-four hours, an estimated 20,000 armed citizens from all over the state descended on Boston to defend its inhabitants. When word filtered down that Gage had embarked only on a minor mission, everyone headed back to their homes.

They had acted on simply a rumor.

* * *

While it was clear that the American people were ready to fight for their freedom, it was equally clear that the British government seemed intent on taking over the reins of authority and power. In the process, America's prosperous economy was in danger of being destroyed; its citizens persecuted and taxed to death; and the people's individual rights, personal property, and colonial territories taken from them.

What were they to do?

The Americans were David against the mighty Goliath of Great Britain—whose empire was the strongest economic power on earth with the largest and most powerful navy and army. The Americans had no army, no navy, no kings or queens to look to for leadership. And there were no precedents for a colony breaking away from its parent country to form a new and independent nation. It simply had never before been done. How were the Americans to overcome such overwhelming odds?

Clearly, the American people needed leadership. But new leaders would have to rise from within their own ranks—which is exactly what happened. As a matter of fact, history regards the crisis of the American Revolution as having produced some of the greatest captains of true leadership that civilization has ever known.

Well, that begs a fundamental question: Just what exactly is true leadership, anyway? And how does it differ from, say, management or dictatorship?

In his landmark book *Leadership*, James MacGregor Burns offered a simple and clear definition that, with slight modification, is an excellent starting point:

> Leadership is leaders acting—as well as caring, inspiring and persuading others to act—for certain shared goals that represent the values—the wants and needs, the aspirations and expecta-

tions—of themselves and the people they represent. And the genius of leadership lies in the manner in which leaders care about, visualize, and act
on their own and their followers' values and mo-
tivations.

There are three key points to remember about this definition. First, leadership omits the use of coercive power. Leaders, rather, move others by caring, by inspiring, and by
persuading. While tyranny and dictatorship are not only contradictory to the rights of human nature, they are contradictory to leadership itself. Second, leaders have a bias for action
that is centered around shared goals. And third, leaders act
with respect to the values of the people they represent—
which are in concert with their own personal convictions.

True leadership, then, is very different from many theories
of modern management that are centered around a command and control hierarchy. Furthermore, compromise, consensus, and teamwork (so-called soft management
techniques) vault to the forefront. Why? Because if leaders
are to act for the people they represent, they must first listen,
establish trust, discuss, debate, understand, and learn. Effective communication also becomes critical because it is the
only way to inspire and persuade others.

There has always been difficulty in understanding and
practicing real leadership. That's because it is more of an art
than a process. There seem to be no set rules for leaders to
follow—only guidelines and concepts, perceptions and ideas,
abstractions and generalities.

So how do we learn to be effective leaders? We learn by observing successful individuals, by studying those who have
demonstrated their abilities with tangible, visceral results.
When studying great leaders of the past, consistent patterns
begin to emerge; common skills become readily apparent;
and certain personal traits appear and reappear time after
time—from leader to leader, from century to century.

By careful observation, it becomes apparent that effective leadership requires specific skills and abilities. For example, good leaders are visionary and decisive. They are able to effectively communicate both their vision and their decisions to a wide array of people, in a variety of venues with multiple methods. Effective leaders have an intuitive understanding of human nature that combines with the ability to care, establish trust, and build alliances. They are able to work in teams, which, in turn, leads to exceptional skills in fashioning consensus, compromising when necessary, and valuing diversity of thought, ability, and culture. Also, the best leaders have the know-how to successfully create and manage change.

In addition to these acquired abilities, truly great leaders tend to exhibit certain personal traits that are more a part of their character, more innate. They include: high ethical standards in which a person consistently attempts to "do the right thing"; an unusually strong bias for action fueled by a high rate of personal energy and an almost uncontrollable desire to achieve; and a propensity for lifelong learning, curiosity, and continual improvement. Many leaders also possess an unwavering self-confidence that frequently translates into courage in the face of adversity, the willingness to take risks, and a sense of destiny—a personal belief that they are meant for something special, perhaps even greatness.

Moreover, the study of acknowledged great leaders has produced solid evidence that people can be predisposed to creative and effective leadership from childhood. For instance, many past leaders experienced a strong bond with their mothers. For some, this connection was accompanied by an overwhelmingly negative or virtually nonexistent attachment to their fathers—completing a true oedipal relationship.

Howard Gardner, in his book *Leading Minds*, noted that: "Future leaders have often lost fathers at an early age. According to one study, over 60 percent of major British political leaders lost a parent in childhood, more often the father."

He also confirmed that leaders often experienced "a contrasting set of relations with their parents" and that, at an early age, they displayed "confidence" and "a willingness to rely on oneself."

Certainly this was true of Abraham Lincoln, for instance, who had an exceptionally close relationship with his stepmother. The depth of their unusually warm bond was illustrated when Lincoln visited her just prior to assuming the presidency. She had been his earliest and strongest source of reassurance and support. By contrast, Lincoln refused to even attend his father's funeral.

Franklin Roosevelt had a well-known attachment to his mother—and was frequently referred to as a "mama's boy." Because of bouts of chronic illness, Theodore Roosevelt maintained a strikingly physical attachment to his mother, who, in childhood, seemed to be always by his side. Even Sigmund Freud—the great psychiatrist and leader of the psychoanalysis movement—received special attention from his mother, while feeling ambivalent toward his father. That may have led, in part, to his famous observation in *The Interpretation of Dreams*: "I have found," wrote Freud, "that people who know that they are preferred or favored by their mother give evidence in their lives of a peculiar self-reliance and an unshakable optimism which often seem like heroic attributes and bring actual success to their possessors."

Many future leaders also experienced some form of tragedy relatively early in life. Mohandas K. Gandhi lost his father in adolescence. At the age of nine, Lincoln experienced the death of his natural mother, and when he was nineteen, his sister died in childbirth. Theodore Roosevelt lost his father when he was nineteen, and six years later, his mother and wife died on the same day. Franklin Roosevelt was barely eighteen when his father passed away—and the burning death of his aunt when he was two years of age may have accounted for his lifelong fear of fire.

Sickness and death experienced by these well-known leaders may have led to a feeling that life is short; there's not much time to achieve; better make the most of it while you're here on this earth. Many contemporaries reported that these men always seemed to have more energy than the average person—were always busy and seemed to be in a hurry.

Countless leaders grew up in a home that had a strong work ethic and high moral values—one where books and learning were not only encouraged but commonplace. Theodore Roosevelt's home was a place of habitual learning and constant reinforcement. His father always encouraged him to seize the moment. Lincoln, when young, was rarely without a book. Harry Truman's parents admonished him to be good, urged hard work down on the farm, and reinforced the belief that he could be anything he wanted to be. Later in life, Truman recalled never being bored because "we had a house full of books."

Compare this profile with those of some of the more famous American founding fathers. There was the unbridled curiosity and intellectual capacity of Benjamin Franklin, Thomas Jefferson, and James Madison. There was the self-confidence and sense of destiny felt by both George Washington and John Adams. All were known for their integrity, courage, and high moral values. All were continual learners who surrounded themselves with books of all kinds. And, without exception, all were achievement-oriented, energetic, and driven.

Many of the founding fathers had very close relationships with their mothers coupled with a strained or nonexistent relationship with their fathers. As a matter of fact, several experienced their father's death relatively early in life: Jefferson was fourteen years old when his father died; Washington only eleven. The Marquis de Lafayette's father was killed when he was two years old. Alexander Hamilton's father abandoned his family when the boy was ten—and John Adams lost his father at the age of twenty-six. As such, while coming from many different backgrounds, with varied upbringings, the founding fathers also turned out to have many things in common.

At the dawn of the American Revolution, Europeans viewed America as a backwoods wilderness—and Americans themselves as colonial bumpkins, inferior in stature and intelligence. The British empire attempted to impose both political and business tyranny on the American colonies. But the local people drew together in support of one idea: the idea that humankind had a right to be free, to have a say in their own affairs, with a right to self-government.

History has shown that especially effective leaders tend to emerge during periods of great change. For every turning point in American history, a creative leader—right for the times and uniquely suited to the task—took the helm: Abraham Lincoln during the Civil War; Franklin Roosevelt during the Great Depression and World War II; Harry Truman in its aftermath; and Dr. Martin Luther King, Jr. during the American Civil Rights movement.

At a most crucial moment in time, the great men now renowned as America's founding fathers rose from the masses to lead the people of their homeland. They acted as a team—preparing for the Revolution, winning the war, and following through after victory was achieved. At appropriate times, when their individual skills, knowledge, and expertise were needed, some assumed the role of team leaders—then stepped back when another phase necessitated the need for others to be out in front.

What made these men different from everyone else—and what were their similarities? Where did they come from? Why did they step forward? And how did they lead a revolution of both war and thought that eventually created a new nation with a new form of government that, in turn, provided new hope for the future of humankind?

The leadership principles employed by the founding fathers still apply today—in business, in politics, and in life. Those tenets are outlined in the following pages.

This is their story—of unselfish, genuine leadership.

This is their legacy.

PART I
PREPARING FOR THE REVOLUTION

"The Administration has totally lost all sense and feeling of morality [and is] governed by passion, cruelty and revenge."

Samuel Adams,
May 18, 1774

"Give me liberty, or give me death."

Patrick Henry,
March 23, 1775

"The British are coming. The British are coming."

Paul Revere,
April 18, 1775

1 / *Sound the Trumpet*

TEAM LEADERS
Samuel Adams
Patrick Henry
Paul Revere

By being out in front and taking people where they've never before been, leaders essentially act as agents of change. And yet, in what is a fundamental tendency of human nature, people often react emotionally, with trepidation and anxiety, when presented with an unknown future. Accordingly, the best leaders know that before great numbers of people can be moved to act, they first must be informed of facts and information regarding current affairs—and then *persuaded* as to why they should consider changing.

In essence, the first step in the change process involves raising awareness. And that's exactly what the founding fathers did. Their initial actions revolved around getting their messages out by a spontaneous natural process, by design, and by necessity.

Initial dissent usually arises from one or two small pockets of passion—both individually and geographically. The first people to take hard stands are those who are directly affected by events, who are risk-takers, who are something of inbred revolutionaries.

One of the first great American rabble-rousers was Samuel Adams. A native of Boston and educated at Harvard, Adams grew up in a strict moral household. His father, a justice of the peace busy in local politics, died when Sam was twenty-six, leaving the young man with a heavy amount of debt. A failed businessman himself, Adams spent ten years prior to the Stamp Act employed by the city of Boston as a tax collector. While he seemed to be mediocre in most of his professional endeavors, Sam Adams was an energetic, driven man whose outrage at British tyranny turned quickly to radical activism.

He was a powerful force well before the British placed his hometown under siege. Having been shocked and appalled by the sheer injustice of the Intolerable Acts, he accused the British of having "totally lost all sense and feeling of morality," and of being motivated "by passion, cruelty and revenge." "For flagrant injustice and barbarity," Adams wrote to a friend in 1774, "one might search in vain among the archives of [history] to find a match for it."

Much of the general public quickly labeled Adams a fanatic—even something of a lunatic. But others admired the fact that he was passionate and had a vision for America's destiny. "We are not what we should be," he said. "We should labor for the future [rather] than for the present moment."

Today, Sam Adams is known as the "Father of the American Revolution." He organized the Sons of Liberty—a group of mostly small businessmen, printers, and lawyers whose livelihood stood in grave danger by British attempts to control the American economic system. Their mission, said Adams, was "to frustrate the diabolical designs of our enemies."

In turn, Sam Adams and the Sons of Liberty instigated the Boston Tea Party where they met under a newly created flag—a green tree on a white background with the words "Liberty Tree" and "Appeal to God." Adams was nearly sixty years old when he became the first to call for the formation of a Continental Congress—of which he served as a member until 1781. While seldom speaking in session, he was known for his constant demand that the people have a say in their government's affairs. "A state is never free but when each citizen is bound by no law whatever that he has not approved of," Adams advocated.

In what was perhaps his most significant contribution to the American cause, in the summer of 1772 Adams persuaded the Boston Town Meeting to form a Committee of Correspondence for the purpose of disseminating information. The committee's goals were to "state the rights of the colonists," to document "the violations thereof," and to "communicate and publish."

Within a month, the new committee produced what quickly became known as the "Boston Pamphlet." It was essentially a statement of rights and grievances that included written attacks on the British for tyranny and unwarranted taxation. The committee printed 600 copies, which found their way to every nook and cranny of Massachusetts. In turn, many towns were inspired to form their own committees of correspondence.

If Sam Adams was a rabble-rouser, he also became a focal point for new ideas and the persistent pursuit of those ideas. He instigated an entirely new movement of propagandist literature that inspired others to persevere, to speak out, and, ultimately, to take action. "Calmness, courage and unanimity prevail," he wrote in 1774. "The people persist."

In Adams's wake, other future founding fathers began to

make their voices heard by writing materials similar to the Boston Pamphlet. Down in Virginia, Thomas Jefferson made himself a leading revolutionary figure when, in 1774, he published *A Summary View of the Rights of British America*. In this scathing attack on the Crown, Jefferson declared that "George III had no right to land a single armed man on our shores," and that kings are the "servants, not the proprietors of the people." He outlined the rights of Americans "as the common rights of mankind," and appealed to British citizens that "all such assumptions of unlawful power are dangerous to the right of the British empire in general."

In New York, Alexander Hamilton penned a series of pamphlets attacking the policies of Great Britain. In Massachusetts, John Adams (younger cousin of Sam Adams) published a series of letters in the *Massachusetts Gazette*, under the pen name "Novanglus," entitled "The Rule of Law and the Rule of Men." And in Philadelphia, Thomas Paine wrote countless articles, stories, and, in 1775, this well-known poem:

> *From the east to the west blow the trumpet to arms!*
> *Through the land let the sound of it flee.*
> *Let the far and the near all unite, with a cheer,*
> *In defense of our Liberty Tree.*

The south's early dissent was led not only by Thomas Jefferson, who was more of an intellectual thinker than a fanatic, it was also led by a Virginia rabble-rouser named Patrick Henry. He was the southern version of Sam Adams—an emotional agitator, a driven activist.

Henry's father was a hard-drinking church vestryman, and his mother a warm religious woman devoted to her family. His formal education ended when he was fifteen in part because his parents could not afford to pay for any further studies. Early on, Henry demonstrated an ability to touch ordinary people with plain talk. In front of large groups, he was often mesmerizing and spoke with passion and confidence. Considered a quick learner, he tried a variety of ways to earn a living. He was a clerk, a farmer, an innkeeper, a bartender, and a failed businessman. Eventually, he taught himself the law, became a successful lawyer, entered politics, and served in the Virginia Assembly, the Virginia House of Burgesses, and the Continental Congress. He also became a three-term governor of Virginia and, afterward, served in the state legislature.

In the decade prior to the war, Patrick Henry was a tireless voice in advocating open rebellion against the Crown. Like Sam Adams, he was one of the first to call for a Continental Congress—and he persevered through years of contentious debate against his own radical ideas.

On March 23, 1775, the one hundred or more members of the Virginia House of Burgesses convened in Richmond to discuss security measures for the colony and, possibly, to elect delegates to the upcoming Continental Congress. The meeting was held in a small wooden building, the Henrico Parish Church, because it was the only place in town large enough to seat all the members.

By this time, General Gage had directed action against leaders of the American colonies. All the members knew of the plight of the Bostonians, and that to take any concrete action against the Crown could be labeled treason. But Patrick Henry, at the age of thirty-eight, had no fear—and he came to the assembly prepared. Almost immediately, he entered a motion that Virginia draft a plan "for embodying, arming, and disciplining a number of men" for the purpose of "defense." After many of the members voiced serious opposition and charged that he was going too far, that there was still hope for reconciliation with Great Britain, Henry rose to defend his position. Seated in the crowded pews that day were Thomas Jefferson, Richard Henry Lee and his three brothers—and one Colonel George Washington.

"Mr. President," began Henry, "it is natural to man to indulge in the illusions of hope. . . . [But] are we disposed to be of the number of those who, having eyes, see not, and having ears, hear not?"

He then asked what, judging by "the lamp of experience," the British had done in the last ten years to give the people any hope. "Are fleets and armies necessary to a work of love and reconciliation?" asked Henry. "Let us not deceive ourselves [any] longer. These are the last arguments to which kings resort.

"They tell us that we are weak," he continued, "unable to cope with so formidable an adversary. But when shall we be stronger? . . . Three millions of people, armed in the holy cause of liberty, and in such a country as that which we possess, are invincible by any force which our enemy can send against us.

"The battle is not to the strong alone; it is to the vigilant, the active, the brave," advocated Henry. And then, referring to British tyranny in Massachusetts, he said: "Our chains are forged. Their clanking may be heard on the plains of Boston! . . . Our brethren are already in the field!

"Why stand we here idle?" concluded Henry with a flourish. "What is it that gentlemen wish? What would they have? Is life so dear, or peace so sweet, as to be purchased at the price of chains and slavery? Forbid it, Almighty God! I know not what course others may take; but as for me, give me liberty, or give me death!"

After several moments of stunned silence, the delegates entered into a lengthy debate. Patrick Henry's motion passed by a margin of only five votes—and Virginia created its militia (of which Henry eventually became commander in chief). But the words spoken that day had a much more far-reaching impact. Patrick Henry's call to arms was echoed by revolutionaries all across the thirteen colonies and many citizens prepared to fight. Furthermore, his words would remain a source of inspiration all throughout the war as some soldiers had lettered on the fronts of their shirts the slogan "Liberty or Death."

Meantime, Henry had also incited the British to act.

who were in Lexington (eleven miles northwest of Boston), and then move on to seize military supplies at Concord, six miles farther west.

On April 18, 1775, Gage moved quietly so as not to raise any suspicions. After issuing instructions for strict secrecy, he prepared his troops to cross the harbor by ship and then move to Lexington and Concord under the cover of darkness. At ten o'clock that night, officers were ordered to wake their men by calmly shaking them and then have them move quietly through the streets in small groups.

But the British precautions for secrecy were too late. Earlier that afternoon, citizens noticed some unusual activity on the warships in Boston Harbor—and that a number of British officers were whispering quietly to themselves. A few drunken navy seamen were overheard in a bar, and a stable boy had eavesdropped on two officers and heard one of them say that there would be "hell to pay tomorrow."

Word quickly reached Dr. Warren, who, after confirming Gage's intentions through other informers, immediately summoned Paul Revere and another patriot, William Dawes. He relayed the information and, in case one did not get through, gave both men the same written message. It read: "A large body of the King's troops (supposed to be a brigade of about 12, or 1500) were embarked in boats from Boston, and gone to land at Lechmere's point."

Immediately, Revere passed the word to his comrades to light two lanterns in the steeple window—which was done for only a few brief minutes. It was, however, long enough for the appointed spotters in Charlestown to see the lights flickering. While Revere got in a rowboat and crossed the bay, the spotters prepared his horse.

The forty-year-old Revere was unarmed and dressed like a gentleman when he left for Lexington. Riding at a full gallop most of the way, he was nearly captured by one of the many parties of British troops sent out by General Gage to stop any express riders who might have gotten wind of the movement.

At just after midnight, Revere arrived and pounded on the front door of the Clarke residence where Adams and Hancock were staying. Having been roused from sleep, both leaders soon popped their heads out of downstairs windows. Dawes, traveling on a different path, arrived a few minutes later. The patriot leaders had been given sufficient warning to escape.

Both riders then headed off to warn the town of Concord. While Dawes made it, Revere did not. He was surrounded by about ten soldiers and captured. One of them, Revere recalled, "clapped a pistol to my head and said he was going to ask me some questions, and if I did not tell the truth, he would blow my brains out." After learning that they were probably too late to stop an advanced warning for Lexington and Concord, the British released Revere, but kept his horse. He then walked the several miles back to Lexington and personally escorted Hancock and Adams to safety.

Paul Revere's midnight ride was not a solitary one as has been widely recounted. Rather it was part of a much larger effort that involved hundreds of people. At the time, it was renowned as the night of the "Lexington Alarm." Church bells rang in Boston and the persistent beat of drums could be heard through the night along the north shore of Massachusetts Bay. Signal fires and the sound of muskets roused the town of Carlisle. A slave named Abel Benson awoke part of the town of Needham by blowing his trumpet. And Paul Revere, as he said himself, "alarmed almost every house, till I got to Lexington," sometimes, as legend has it, by yelling: "The British are coming. The British are coming."

The Lexington Alarm warned people up to twenty miles outside Boston of the impending British action. The route to Lexington was covered in three hours; Concord was alerted within five hours; and the rest of the area in less than ten. The system had worked and, what's more, the American patriots carried out their plans between the hours of 11:00 P.M. and 9:30 A.M.—almost entirely in total darkness—and without sleep. Neither Paul Revere nor any of the dozens of other express riders and volunteers were paid for their work. They did it because they cared.

Modern leaders can learn a thing or two from Paul Revere and the other American patriots. When people really care about a cause, they will not only act on their own initiative, they'll move mountains to get the job done. "Just tell me what I need to do," they'll often request of their leaders. Therefore, getting the word out, or communicating the need for change, becomes one of the most critical elements in inspiring others to follow. In all organizations, the difference between leaders and mere managers is understanding this basic principle.

True leadership also rests in the understanding that people do not like being ordered around or told what to do. They would rather feel a part of the process, that their contributions really do make a difference, that they are part of a team—rather than only a servant or an employee.

Confronted with a dictatorial situation in corporate America, for instance, people may not openly say what's on their minds, but they will speak to each other about their feelings. Whispers in the hallway, in the restrooms, and in the cafeteria may become part of a larger rumor mill until perception becomes reality in the minds of many employees—until they become followers no more. And, if things get bad enough, the people will lead a revolt, or look for a new job, rather than submit to oppression. That is especially true in the United States of America, where citizens are born free, and where the Constitution guarantees an individual's rights to be treated fairly.

In the early stages of the American Revolution, Americans rebelled at being taken over without reason, at being ordered about and told what to do—by force and coercion. Because human nature remains the same, people in modern organizations will react just the way eighteenth-century Americans did. If they are victims of a hostile takeover, if they are subjected to a new tyrannical boss, or if they are the continual victims of coercion and oppression—they will rebel.

Within minutes of Paul Revere's arrival in town, 130 armed members of the Lexington militia, led by Captain John Parker, followed their emergency instructions to the tee and gathered on Lexington Green. Sentries were sent out on horseback to watch for the British approach. Captain Parker then asked his men to wait for a drum signal at nearby Buckman's Tavern—out of the cold night air, so they'd be rested and fresh for a potential engagement. Meanwhile, Paul Revere returned to town to retrieve John Hancock's trunk, which was filled with secret American papers.

At 4:30 A.M. on the morning of April 19, 1775, one of the sentries, Thaddeus Bowman, galloped in with the news that British troops were approaching. The drum sounded immediately and Parker aligned his men in two ranks along the border of Lexington Green—positioned directly between the British and the road to Concord.

When the British troops arrived at the dawn's first light, they were tense. All through the night they had heard the shots, the bells, the drums, the riders' hoofbeats. They knew that the entire countryside had been warned. Dressed in impressive uniforms and armed with rifles and bayonets, they outnumbered the Americans by a margin of three or four to one. The militia, by contrast, were a ragtag lot armed with whatever old muskets and pistols they had lying around.

"Stand your ground!" Captain Parker said as he turned to his men. "Don't fire unless fired upon! But if they want to have a war let it begin here!"

"Throw down your arms, you damned rebels!" shouted a British officer to the Minute Men.

The two armies stood toe-to-toe for a few tense moments.

Suddenly, the silence was broken as a shot rang out. It would later be known as the "shot heard 'round the world"—and both sides would claim the other had fired first.

Then, as Paul Revere later described, there was "the continual roar of musketry" as the British opened fire. When the redcoats charged, the militia broke and ran. They were no match for British regulars, and they were scared to death.

The battle was over in a matter of minutes. The Americans suffered eighteen casualties (eight dead, ten wounded); the British only one lightly injured. British soldiers cheered and shouted at their victory, which only served to further anger the townspeople of Lexington.

Several hours later, Captain Parker and the militia regrouped, this time joined by more men arriving from the outer countryside. And later that day, when the British resumed their march to Concord, they were ambushed by several hundred Minute Men at the North Bridge of the Concord River. Time and time again during this battle, the Americans nipped at the British by sneaking up on them individually or in small groups. Using whatever ground cover was available, they fired their muskets and then quickly ran away. It was the only tactic they could think of that would work against so formidable a foe.

In the weeks and months that followed, occupied Boston erupted into a guerrilla war zone. American snipers fired at the British from their homes; there were armed skirmishes in the streets; and the frustrated redcoats burned houses and killed anyone they were able to catch in arms.

As American militiamen surrounded the city, the British fortified their garrison. "Our situation [here in Boston] is beyond description," wrote Massachusetts Chief Justice Peter Oliver to a friend on June 1, 1775.

The American Revolution had officially begun.

THE FOUNDING FATHERS ON LEADERSHIP

★ The first step in the change process involves raising awareness.

★ You should labor for the future rather than only for the present moment.

★ People are bound by no law whatever that they have not approved of.

★ Touch ordinary people with plain talk and be a good public speaker.

★ *Have* no fear, and *show* no fear.

★ Success will not belong to the strong alone—but to the vigilant, the active, and the brave.

★ Do not stand idle. When will you be stronger?

★ Create an effective network of communications that will disseminate accurate information quickly.

★ Be prepared for even the worst-case scenario.

★ Human nature is such that all people will rebel when subjected to continual coercion and oppression.

★ It's okay to use cover and sneak up on an overwhelming competitor.

> "[I see] a union and a confederation of thirteen states, independent of Parliament, of Minister and of King!"
>
> John Adams, 1774
>
> ─────────
>
> "[We should] invite the people to erect the whole building with their own hands, upon the broadest foundation. . . . For the people [are] the source of all authority and power."
>
> John Adams, 1774

2 / Create a Vision, Set Goals, and Involve Everyone

| TEAM LEADER
| John Adams

Just as a skilled craftsman envisions a finished product before beginning work, a creative leader usually has a pretty good idea of where he wants to go before acting or attempting to inspire others to act. As such, vision is at the heart of leadership. For every one person who sees, thousands may think. And for the thousands who think, millions may act.

Effective visions provide context, give purpose, and establish meaning. They inspire people to mobilize and move in the same general direction. And once an accepted vision is implemented, a consensus builds that often results in enhanced understanding of the organization's overall mission.

All the best modern thinking on leadership emphasizes the need for leaders to have some sort of vision. Stephen R. Covey wrote in *Principle-Centered Leadership* that successful leaders "begin with the end in mind"; that people are "more in need of a vision and less in need of a road map"; and that an effective vision "creates a context that gives meaning, direction, and coherence to everything. . . ." In addition, Tom Peters, in *Thriving on Chaos*, noted that an effective vision is not only inspiring, but "clear and challenging—and about excellence." A vision should be able to make sense and stand the test of time; remain stable, yet flexible. It empowers people and prepares for the future while having roots in the past.

In creating and gaining widespread acceptance of their visions, leaders provide the only effective mechanism that can truly overcome the natural human tendency to resist change. Once everyone has bought in, people begin to set goals to achieve the vision. They're mobilized, they're acting—they're *changing*. No longer is there fear of the unknown. Fear and resistance are replaced by purpose, by excitement, by desire, by courage—and by action.

Even though, as Howard Gardner stated in *Leading Minds*, "the rarest individual is the leader who creates a new story," and that "visionary leaders are extreme rarities," several of the founding fathers could be considered as such. However, John Adams seemed to have a new story and a vision that was just a bit grander, a bit more clear. Moreover, he was one of the first to passionately articulate a single idea that would ultimately unite all the colonies.

Born and raised in humble circumstances in the small village of Braintree, Massachusetts, Adams never lost the gift of being grounded in the realities of common people. His father worked as a farmer and a shoemaker and his mother instilled in him a strict Christian upbringing. An avid reader and lifelong learner, Adams was educated a lawyer and resolved never to "suffer one hour to pass unimproved. . . . I will rouse up my mind and fix my attention," he wrote. "I will stand collected within myself and think upon what I read and what I see."

John Adams was compassionate, caring, and had a tremendous sense of honesty and integrity—sometimes even to a fault, observed his friends, because he seemed to be outraged at even the slightest injustice. After Lexington and Concord, for instance, he argued passionately that "if we did not defend ourselves they would kill us." And he warned British officials that people would not be "ridden like horses, and fleeced like sheep, and worked like cattle, and fed and clothed like hogs and hounds."

Despite being a rather shy individual, Adams was a forceful public speaker. In public life, he was known for his unselfish attitude and the courage to take on established traditions. But he also had a thin skin. Prone to spells of depression, he was very sensitive to perceived or real attacks on his character.

John Adams was creative, imaginative, persistent—and driven to achieve. "It is my destiny," he wrote when still a young man, "to dig treasures with my own fingers." And yet he also had a generous dose of humility. Pondering his future after being elected to the Congress, Adams recorded in his diary: "There is a new and grand scene open before me. I feel myself unequal to this business. I am but an ordinary man. The times alone have destined me to fame."

In May 1774, in the wake of the Intolerable Acts, the Virginia House of Burgesses (meeting in the Raleigh Tavern at Williamsburg) advocated an immediate gathering of representatives from all the colonies. The next month, Sam Adams introduced a resolution in the Massachusetts House of Representatives also calling for such a meeting on the first day of September. When the motion passed, Governor General Gage immediately declared the legislature dissolved.

Operating on a one-colony, one-vote rule, fifty-five representatives convened the First Continental Congress (on September 5) for seven weeks in Philadelphia. Almost immediately, the delegates divided into action-oriented radicals hell-bent on changing their relationship with Great Britain—and more timid conservatives who, because they tended to be businessmen with strong economic ties to Great Britain, preferred diplomatic talks.

Sensing an immense opportunity, John Adams seized the moment and emerged to lead the charge of the radicals. But he began delicately and quietly. Having been a scholar of the scriptures, he may have read the verse "Write the vision, and make it plain upon the table, that he may run that readeth it." As such, Adams communicated his vision simply. He merely began whispering to the other delegates the word "independence." It was simple, everyone understood it, and everyone thought about it. Soon it was on the lips of many representatives until it became their own idea—not just that of John Adams.

Eventually, the idea was introduced in open debate by Adams, who said: "The Cancer [of British tyranny] is too deeply rooted, and too far spread to be cured by anything short of cutting it out entirely. Nothing can save us," he said, "but discipline in the army, governments in every colony, and a confederation of the whole." And finally, John Adams said, in no uncertain terms, what he really foresaw: "A union and a confederation of thirteen states, independent of Parliament, of Minister and of King!"

His thoughtful, action-oriented ways began to have a positive effect on delegates—and, as a result, his reputation spread throughout the colonies. As a matter of fact, even North Carolina's ultra-conservative legislature recommended to its delegates that, in the event independence was declared, they should "apply to Mr. John Adams of Massachusetts for his views on the form of government they should assume."

Then the other members of Congress asked him to draft a "Declaration of Rights" for the American colonies. On October 14, his document was adopted. It began, simply enough: "That the inhabitants of the English Colonies in North America, by the laws of nature . . . have the following rights. . . ." And then he listed ten points, beginning with the most basic of human rights. "They are entitled," wrote Adams, "to life, liberty, and property, and they have never ceded to any sovereign power whatever, a right to dispose of either without their consent."

His tenth and final point, by design, would leave no room for mistaking the American position regarding Great Britain's oppressive actions. "The constituent branches of the legislature [are] independent of each other," he began, "therefore, the exercise of legislative power in several colonies by a council appointed by the crown is unconstitutional, dangerous, and destructive to the freedom of American legislation."

Once his vision began to draw support and acceptance among the delegates of the First Continental Congress, Adams might have backed off and let the message run by itself. But he didn't. Rather he took his strategy for implementation one step higher by advocating not only the involvement of the delegates themselves, but the collective involvement of all people with "intelligence, curiosity, and enterprise.

"[We should] invite the people to erect the whole building with their own hands, upon the broadest foundation," Adams advised. "[Congress should recommend] to the people of every colony to call conventions of representatives . . . and set up governments of their own, under their own authority; for the people [are] the source of all authority and power."

Such an idea was so extreme that even most of his fellow radicals couldn't see it. And even though Adams cautioned patience, saying that the people were an "unwieldy machine" and could not be forced, his motion was tabled indefinitely. The American people, however, did not wait for Congress's approval. Most of the colonies spontaneously formed illegal committees specifically designed to take the functions of their government back from the British.

By calling for involvement of a wide array of people, John Adams was advocating one of the most basic premises of effective leadership. He realized that if Congress told people what to do, then the outcome would be the responsibility of Congress. However, if they inspired others to act on their own accord, the responsibility and results would be the people's. Adams's idea also hinted at the basis for teamwork. With more people involved, there would be more ideas, more participation, a better outcome—and, ultimately, more action to achieve the vision.

After Congress adjourned at the end of October the radical leaders continued to plan and strategize. For instance, Adams, in Massachusetts, stayed in constant contact with Patrick Henry of Virginia. Both felt that it was important to set a series of overarching goals to prepare for an impending conflict with Great Britain that would eventually lead to their shared vision of independence for the colonies.

In early 1775, John Adams placed his initial goals down on paper in a memorandum to his colleagues. This list included:

- Raising a substantial military force;
- Increasing production of gunpowder;
- Wresting the city of Boston from British control;
- Forming a military and economic alliance with France and Spain;
- Dispatching emissaries to both nations;
- Signing shipping treaties with Holland and Denmark;
- Levying taxes to support the cause;
- Regulating colonial coins and currency;
- Passing legislation that declared British shipping fair game to American privateers;
- Issuing a formal declaration of independence; and
- Declaring war on Great Britain.

Why did John Adams lay out so many goals? Were they really necessary? Did they serve any purpose? Recall the definition of leadership: *Leaders act for certain goals that represent the values—the wants and needs, the aspirations and expectations—of the people they represent.* Establishing goals and gaining their acceptance are both indispensable and crucial for effective leadership. Goals unify people, motivate them, focus their talent and energy. Moreover, goals help a person, or an organization, *achieve* things. Striving toward a clear objective facilitates progress and fosters decisiveness.

Adams's list of goals came in very handy when the Second Continental Congress met in Philadelphia three weeks after the fighting at Lexington and Concord. It was May 10, 1775, and most moderates and many conservatives in Congress were completely outraged at the British aggression. Also, virtually everyone agreed that there was now an urgent need to do *something*.

Adams's list became the vehicle behind which the Congress mobilized. A series of committees were immediately established to solicit loans, raise money, and secure and produce gunpowder. John Adams moved to adopt the militia surrounding Boston as a Continental Army. A resolution was also passed to raise six companies of riflemen from Pennsylvania, Maryland, and Virginia.

Another committee (comprised of Thomas Jefferson, Benjamin Franklin, John Dickinson, and John Jay) was charged with composing a document in justification of raising and arming troops. Jefferson penned the first draft, the others refined it and, on July 6, 1775, the "Declaration of the Causes and Necessities of Taking Up Arms" was passed by Congress. "We are reduced to the alternative of choosing an unconditional submission to the tyranny of irritated ministers, or resistance by force," the delegates had written. "Our cause is just. . . . We fight not for glory or for conquest. We exhibit to mankind the remarkable spectacle of a people attacked by unprovoked enemies, without imputation or even suspicion of offenses."

Not long thereafter, Congress voted to raise an army of 20,000 men and called for the purchase of muskets, bayonets, and other arms. John Adams, realizing that the colonies were at a serious disadvantage on the open seas, further proposed that an American navy be established. All commerce and economics were dependent on shipping and Great Britain had the mightiest navy in the world. Accordingly, Congress formed the Marine Committee, consisting of one member from each colony, with direct responsibility to organize, outfit, and direct operations of an American naval force.

And Benjamin Franklin (who had been nominated to Congress the day after returning to Philadelphia from London) drew up another document, which he called a preliminary "Articles of Confederation and Perpetual Union." It was approved by Jefferson and presented to Congress for consideration as a means of leading up to future passage of a declaration of independence.

In a first attempt to meet their goal of creating successful foreign alliances, Congress established a committee, chaired by Franklin, "for the sole purpose of corresponding with our friends in Great Britain, Ireland, and other parts of the world." The group called themselves the Committee of Secret Correspondence and by the end of 1775, they had appointed Arthur Lee, Pennsylvania's agent in London, a full-fledged member of their committee with instructions to build local relationships in Europe. The Second Continental Congress also armed privateers and authorized them to seize British ships, instituted an embargo on British trade with the West Indies, and declared open all American ports to all nations *except* Great Britain.

While preparing for the worst, the founding fathers were also hoping for the best. At the same time they were making plans to achieve their goals, they petitioned King George III for peaceful reconciliation. John Dickinson drafted the letter, which, in part, read: "[We] desire that the former harmony between Great Britain and these colonies may be restored. . . . [Please] procure us relief from our afflicting fears and jealousies . . . in pursuance of a happy and permanent reconciliation."

John Adams, who dubbed this document an "Olive Branch," urged and received its passage by Congress. He and the other radicals were gambling that a refusal from the king and the Parliament would move any final conservative hold-outs in Congress over to their ranks.

The radicals were right. King George III refused even to read the Olive Branch Petition. "The King and his Cabinet," said a British official, "are determined to listen to nothing from the illegal congress, to treat with the colonies only one by one, and in no event to recognize them in any form of association." Then, in a remarkable act of retaliation, the king issued a "Proclamation of Rebellion," labeling the colonies' actions as unlawful and rebellious.

By the time word of the king's decree reached America, hostilities had seriously escalated. All through the previous summer members of the Sons of Liberty took it upon themselves to wage a guerrilla war against Great Britain. In New York, they captured several wagonloads of British arms. And off the coast of Maine they seized two supply ships. The Americans also invaded parts of Canada with limited success—but were driven from Quebec by the redcoats with little trouble.

That summer, there was also a major battle on the outskirts of Boston. On June 17, the same alarm system that had alerted Paul Revere to British activity prior to Lexington got wind that General Gage was planning to occupy Dorchester Heights and the hills on the Charlestown peninsula surrounding Boston. Within twenty-four hours, Colonel William Prescott pulled together a 1,000-man force comprised of two regiments of the Massachusetts militia, a portion of the Connecticut militia, and an artillery company with only two guns. He then led the entire force to Bunker Hill and Breed's Hill—high ground on the peninsula that overlooked Boston Harbor and the Charles River. The men worked through the night, from midnight till dawn, constructing earthwork fortifications and digging trenches for cover.

At first light, British ships opened fire on the patriot positions. When that had little effect, the ships turned their guns on the small village of Charlestown nestled at the base of

Breed's Hill. Nearly the entire town was reduced to ashes. Fortunately, the citizens had been warned in time to evacuate.

British forces then crossed the Charles River on barges. Under the cover of warship guns and land batteries, light infantry, grenadiers, and a battery of Royal Marines landed unopposed on the beaches. The first of the militia to confront the British forces were reinforcements from New Hampshire under the command of Captain John Stark. As the redcoats approached with bayonets drawn, Stark ordered his men to hold their fire until the last possible moment. "Don't fire until you see the whites of their eyes," he is reported to have said. When the enemy was within only a few yards, Captain Stark gave the order to fire. The initial result was a catastrophe for the front line of British troops, who were either slaughtered or forced to retreat.

The redcoats, however, outnumbered the Americans two to one and, during the third assault, the militia ran out of ammunition. Unable to hold their lines, the Americans were overrun and forced into a massive retreat. They suffered significant casualties, including the death of Dr. Joseph Warren, president of the Massachusetts Provincial Congress—and the leader who, with Paul Revere, had developed the Lexington alarm system.

Even though the British had officially won the battle and now occupied the Charlestown peninsula, they had lost nearly half of their attacking force (226 killed and 828 wounded). By contrast, the American losses, while heavy, were much less severe. And, while the British troops were demoralized, the militiamen were proud of their effort. They had stood toe-to-toe with the powerful redcoat army, held their ground, and done well.

By the end of 1775, Great Britain's Parliament, in accordance with the king's wishes, had issued the American Prohibitory Act, which declared all foreign trade with the colonies stopped. In addition, King George hired 18,000 German mercenaries (the Hessians) and dispatched them to

America (as part of a 50,000-man military force) to block colonial ports and seize American ships.

The war had now, in all probability, intensified to a point of no return. The British controlled Canada's fate and they still held Boston. America had no formal army, no victories, and no foreign aid. They had not yet achieved any of their overarching goals. They did, however, still have their vision—more shared and intact than ever. And rather than giving up or caving in, the founding fathers became even more determined to succeed.

Three weeks after the battle of Bunker Hill and Breed's Hill, a renewed Benjamin Franklin penned a letter to William Stratham, his good friend in London. "You are a member of Parliament and one of that majesty which has doomed my country to destruction," he wrote. "You have begun to burn our towns and murder our people. Look upon your hands! They are stained with the blood of your relations! You and I were long friends. You are now my enemy, and I am yours!"

Curiously, though, perhaps thinking of future diplomacy, Franklin did not send the note.

THE FOUNDING FATHERS ON LEADERSHIP

★ Have a pretty good idea of where you want to go before you act or attempt to inspire others.

★ Sense your opportunity and seize the moment.

★ Remember that the people are something of a vast unwieldy machine and cannot be forced into anything.

★ Make your vision simple and clear so that everyone may understand it.

★ Begin communicating your vision slowly and softly so that others may first think it over.

★ Invite the people to participate in your vision—building it with their own hands, on the broadest possible foundation.

★ Remember that, ultimately, the people are the source of all authority and power.

★ Collect your thoughts and set your goals down on paper.

★ Utilize your list of goals as a vehicle for achieving your vision.

★ Organize by forming a variety of committees to achieve your goals.

★ Hope for the best, but prepare for the worst.

★ Don't fire until you see the whites of their eyes.

"An enterprise can never be planned and carried on without abilities [of skilled people]. [And those people must have] principle or they cannot have confidence enough in each other."

John Adams, 1786

"I am persuaded and fully convinced that a permanent standing army [is a necessity]. And I mean one to exist during the war."

George Washington, to Congress,
September 2, 1776

"Submit your sentiments with diffidence. A dictatorial style, though it may carry conviction, is always accompanied with disgust."

George Washington, 1776

3 / Build Your Team and Be Decisive

TEAM LEADERS
John Adams
George Washington

Up to this point, the founding fathers had raised awareness, created a vision, and set some high-level goals. But, while they saw themselves as leaders, each realized that they alone could not achieve their vision. More people with talent, skill, expertise, and drive were needed. A team had to be created—one comprised of individuals who would take risks, act without waiting for direction, and request responsibility rather than avoid it. It was time to move to the next crucial stage of the change process: It was time to pick winners for their team.

Because additional members of the organization become involved, teamwork, in and of itself, vaults to the forefront of leadership. By including others, leaders are acting *"for the wants and needs . . . of the people they represent."* An effective team can be a major factor in overcoming an organization's natural resistance to change precisely because it is comprised of working members of the enterprise who, in turn, become supporters of the cause. An organized group gives reinforced meaning to the adage "People support what they help create."

According to Jon R. Katzenbach and Douglas K. Smith, authors of *The Wisdom of Teams*, the most important advantages of an effective team are: bringing together a broader mix of skills that exceeds those of any single individual; jointly developing and striving toward clear goals; adjusting with greater speed and effectiveness; and more easily building trust and confidence.

When creating a team, the best leaders search for people who know the basic difference between right and wrong; for those who can be depended upon to do the right thing; for those who are honest and sincere, and in possession of simple integrity. Second, they seek out individuals with expertise and competence in a variety of areas. And across the team, a broad aspect of diversity is desired—a diversity of skills, experiences, and cultures. Individuals are also selected based on their ability to work with others to make things happen.

Members of the team that achieved independence from Great Britain volunteered or were chosen over a period of time. But John Adams and other members of the Second Continental Congress realized that their first major selection was critical. A strong-willed decision-maker was needed to lead the war effort—to build, train, inspire, and mobilize an army. A great leader was needed, one who, in and of himself, had the potential to be the best of them all.

Accordingly, on June 15, 1775, John Adams rose from his seat in Congress and nominated George Washington of Virginia for the position of commander in chief of the Continental Army. It was to be, perhaps, the most important decision of the entire American Revolution.

Washington was well known to all the delegates. They remembered that during an adjournment of the First Continental Congress he had returned home to urge constituents to begin military preparations for defense. And members were further impressed at the Second Congress when he volunteered to lead four committees dealing with military matters. Everyone also knew that Washington's commitment to the Revolution was unquestioned. "It is my full intention to devote my life and fortune in the cause we are engaged in, if need be," he had said less than three months before being nominated by Adams.

Ever since the imposition of the Intolerable Acts, Washington had been a leading advocate of using force to gain independence from Great Britain. "Shall we whine and cry for relief," he asked in 1774, "and see one province after another fall prey to despotism . . . ? I think the Parliament of Great Britain hath no more right to put their hands into my pocket, without my consent, than I have to put my hands into yours for money. The line . . . ought to be drawn. The crisis is arrived when we must assert our rights."

But the main qualification for George Washington's nomination was his reputation as a soldier during the French and Indian War. It was said that, at the age of twenty-one, he had fired the first shots of the conflict; and that, in a moment of crisis, he had boldly stepped between the rifles of his own men as they shot at each other—and then turned their anger (and fire) on the enemy. It was also a well-known fact that, on July 9, 1755, Washington was the only officer on horseback to survive the battle of the Monongahela. He had ridden back and forth across the battlefield delivering orders from General Edward Braddock until the general was killed. During the encounter the Indians had tried desperately to shoot Washington. Unable to do so, however, they ceased firing at him, believing he was "under the special guardianship of the Great Spirit." Even Washington himself was amazed: "I had four bullets through my coat," he later wrote to his brother, "and two horses shot under me, yet escaped unhurt, although death was leveling my companions on every side of me!"

It is clear that, from an early age, George Washington demonstrated certain attributes and traits common to great leaders. He was, for instance, a courageous risk-taker. "I heard the bullets whistle," he had written to his mother after his first battle, "and believe me, there is something charming in the sound."

He was a self-made man, a continuous learner. He did not attend college and, in fact, had only about eight years of formal schooling—in large part because his parents could not afford more. But Washington became an avid reader and taught himself many things. At the age of sixteen, he copied down 110 "rules of civility" based on a set composed by French Jesuits. Among the rules were such tenets as: "Every action done in company ought to be done with some sign of respect to those that are present" and "Spit not into the fire." The *New Hampshire Gazette* reported that, in later years, "he has made the art of war his particular study." Washington also served several terms in the Virginia state legislature and was a successful surveyor and planter, not to mention being an avid outdoorsman who excelled at hunting, fishing, boating, and riding. Thomas Jefferson called him "the best horseman of his age."

In early adulthood, he suffered the rejection of his first true love and then the adversity (and personal humiliation) of having to surrender Fort Necessity in Pennsylvania during the French and Indian War. Yet, Washington was also courageous, persistent and tenacious. He attempted to learn from his mistakes, to somehow turn adversity to his advantage. He was known for his high physical energy, for his strength and stamina—needing only a few hours of sleep each night, staying healthy when others fell ill. During the Revolutionary War it was reported that he often stayed on horseback for days at a stretch.

In addition, George Washington possessed a drive to achieve, a passion for action. "It is not sufficient," he wrote, "for a man to be a passive friend and a well-wisher to the cause." Above all, Washington was known for his high moral character—one that included honesty, integrity, compassion, and dignity. He was, according to Abigail Adams (John's wife), also "modest, virtuous, amiable, generous, and brave. . . ." "I do not think vanity is a trait of my character," he once simply stated. Washington further knew the value and power of working together in a team. "[We] can no way assist our cruel enemies more effectually than by making division among ourselves," he wrote in 1776.

Moreover, Washington had a bearing and a countenance that impressed others. At six feet three inches, he stood a head taller than most of those around him. He was a man to be looked up to, a man to be followed.

Politics also played a major role in the selection of George Washington to lead the Continental Army. Up until then, New England (especially Massachusetts) had dominated the movement for independence. But John Adams knew that Virginia, being one of the most radical and powerful of all the colonies, had to be won over if there was to be any chance of a united effort against Great Britain. He also reasoned that the other southern colonies might be more willing to fall in line under a southern commander.

The Second Continental Congress unanimously approved John Adams's motion and awarded Washington a commission with the title of "General and Commander in Chief of the United Colonies." In a simple speech filled with humility and modesty, Washington accepted the appointment. "I do not think myself equal to the command," he said. Congress had also voted him a salary of $500 a month, but he declined it.

"I do not wish to make any profit from it," said Washington graciously. He did, however, agree to keep a record of his expenses throughout the war, for which he was reimbursed.

George Washington was forty-three years old and there was, as yet, no army for him to command other than the loose band of militias encircling Boston. "It has been a kind of destiny that has thrown me upon this service," he wrote to his wife, Martha. "I shall hope that my undertaking it is designed to answer some good purpose."

Concurrent with the appointment of a new commander in chief, Congress also named four other generals to serve with Washington: Charles Lee, Israel Putnam, Philip Schuyler, and Artemas Ward. While most of these men were capable in their own right, they were commissioned largely for political reasons—and also because some of them felt slighted at not receiving the top spot.

But the real genius associated with Congress's decision is that the Washingtons of the world tend to multiply as they carefully choose others in their own image. In essence, George Washington appointed officers with leadership abilities similar to his own—so that he could turn ideas and thoughts into actions far beyond what he could ever hope to achieve by himself.

This so-called ripple effect is not uncommon in the annals of American history. During the Civil War, for example, President Abraham Lincoln finally settled on General Ulysses S. Grant to lead the Union forces. In turn, Grant choose two other aggressive individuals in the persons of Philip Sheridan and William Tecumseh Sherman. Working together, they won the war in about a year's time. Similar appointments were made by Dwight Eisenhower after being chosen by Franklin Roosevelt, and by George Marshall after being tapped by Harry Truman.

With time, General Washington would surround himself with some outstanding officers—most of them young, vibrant, and aggressive. He especially concentrated on selecting leaders with integrity. "In every nomination, I have endeavored to make fitness of character my primary object," he said.

Interestingly enough, the man Washington chose to be his replacement should he be killed or captured was Nathanael Greene, a thirty-three-year-old Quaker from Rhode Island who had no previous military experience. What Greene did possess, however (and Washington recognized it), was an incredible bias for action coupled with an ability to lead men. He was an energetic and resourceful individual who, since the Boston Tea Party in 1773, had been teaching himself about military matters. He devoured manuals studying battle tactics and the procurement of arms and supplies. He read biographies of history's great field generals and especially concentrated on their understanding of human nature and how they motivated men to fight. Moreover, Nathanael Greene was totally and passionately dedicated to the American cause. Throughout the war, he entreated the men in his charge to remember what they were fighting for. He unashamedly reminded them that they were fighting to be free.

Another officer who became almost like a son to Washington was a nineteen-year-old French aristocrat titled the Marquis de Lafayette. One in a long line of European volunteers, Lafayette possessed something extra. He was an idealist moved to fight for the American cause. And he wished, in part, to fight the British and avenge the death of his father, who was killed during the French and Indian War. Immediately upon his arrival in Philadelphia, Lafayette appeared before Congress and offered to serve the American cause at his own expense. He was quickly commissioned a major general and sent to join General Washington's staff. The Marquis de Lafayette would eventually spend more than $200,000 of his personal fortune in support of the American Revolution.

There were many other men who were brought along by General Washington, most notably: Alexander Hamilton, who, at the age of twenty, became his secretary and aide-de-camp; and Benedict Arnold, a future hero at the battles of

Ticonderoga and Saratoga—and, later, a traitor to the American cause.

On Sunday, July 3, 1775, George Washington arrived in the Boston area to assume his post as commander in chief of what he was told was an army of between 18,000 and 20,000 men. Almost immediately, he mounted a horse and rode around to visit the troops. The general found his men loosely scattered in a ring around the city. He also noted that the redcoats had strongly fortified their positions on Bunker Hill and Breed's Hill and that they still controlled the seaways.

But he was surprised to see that the men were, by and large, neither well drilled nor in uniform. As a matter of fact, he could not tell the officers from the enlisted men because they were all dressed differently and quartered in the same tents. Washington described the troops as "a mixed multitude of people . . . under very little discipline, order, or government." But they were also men of some pride and determination. After all, they had not been recruited, they simply rushed to the scene when they heard the Lexington alarm on the evening of April 19. They had dropped everything they were doing and left their families with only their muskets and the clothes on their backs.

The British had somewhere between 10,000 and 12,000 well-trained, well-fed, and well-equipped soldiers occupying Boston. By contrast, when Washington asked for a full head count of the American troops surrounding Boston, he was given a loose estimate that the patriots had about 16,000, of which only 14,000 were actually fit for duty. To make matters worse, these men, Washington soon learned, were short of food, clothing, blankets, tents, muskets, bayonets, gunpowder, and virtually everything else an army needed for subsistence. Nor was there any visible means of obtaining supplies—or any money allocated by Congress to purchase provisions or pay the soldiers' salaries. To top it all off, most of the members of the militias had short-term enlistments that would soon expire. General Washington, then, was faced with the seemingly insurmountable task of keeping the army together (which meant persuading most of the men to reenlist without pay not to mention a guarantee of their next meal) while simultaneously training, disciplining, and molding them into an effective military force.

Almost immediately, Washington wrote Congress pleading for reinforcements and supplies. He was concerned that the British might learn of his problem, launch a major offensive, and end the war before it really began. "I think we are in an extremely dangerous situation!" Washington wrote to his friend and fellow Virginian Richard Henry Lee.

Washington's first actions involved issuing a series of orders designed to shore up the army's defenses and instill some discipline and pride in the troops. Each morning specific orders that he had written out the night before were conveyed to the regiments. The men were to dig trenches, raise ramparts, cut down trees, and, in general, prepare their defensive position in the event of an enemy attack. He ordered that barricades be built at all convenient landing places the British did not hold. And hundreds of sentries were deployed around the clock to keep a watchful eye on the British. Horses were also kept saddled as men slept at their positions with their guns by their sides. In an effort to build pride and patriotism, the new commander in chief flew the first Continental flag on January 1, 1776.

As time passed, Washington gained a quiet and steady optimism. "Confusion and disorder reign in every department," wrote Washington to General Schuyler in New York. "However we mend every day and I flatter myself that in a little time we shall work up these new materials into good stuff."

Washington and his men managed to scrounge enough supplies to subsist, and Congress eventually came through with some money. Moreover, while many of the troops failed to reenlist, more than half of those due to go home decided to stick around. But by February, the redcoats in Boston probably outnumbered the American patriots by several thousand—although the British were not aware of that fact.

In mid-February, General Washington, frustrated by weeks of inactivity, convened a council of war. To his generals, he proposed a daring, all-out surprise attack on the British by sending thousands of men across the frozen bay. The other officers, however, unanimously opposed his plan, arguing the Washington was far too optimistic as to the weakness of the British forces and the capabilities of his own troops. The generals, though, did propose another option that Washington, though disappointed in the rejection of his own strategy, agreed to implement.

Such a council of war was not an unusual event for Washington. Prior to making major decisions, he would usually seek the advice of his most trusted generals. But the length of time it took to come to a decision resulted in some critics referring to him as the "Fabian General," largely because delays and avoidance of major fighting were often the result. Despite the negative comments, Washington maintained his deliberating nature when it came to the most important decisions of the war. A reporter for the *New Hampshire Gazette* once reported on the commander's decision-making process:

> When he has any great object in view, he sends for a few of those officers of whose abilities he has a high opinion, and states his present plan among half a dozen others, to all of which they give their separate judgments; by these means, he gets all their opinion, without divulging his intentions.

George Washington was a leader, not a dictator. "Submit your sentiments with diffidence," he advised. "A dictatorial style, though it may carry conviction, is always accompanied with disgust." During the American Revolution, Washington was actually practicing a classic four-step decision-making process—one that most savvy business leaders would employ more than two hundred years later in corporate America. First, he would gather information and understand all the facts involved. Second, he would discuss and review a variety of possible solutions, and try to arrive at a consensus. Third, he would consider the consequences and impact of the decision, and ensure consistency with administrative and personal policy objectives. And fourth, he would effectively communicate the decision—and implement.

Even though Washington had not succeeded in persuading his council of war to execute his pet plan, he had moved the needle, so to speak. He wanted the British out of Boston—which was not only his goal, but the goal of the Continental Congress. Action was what he wanted—and action is what he got.

The other generals suggested that they take the high ground south of Boston, fortify it, and try to draw the British out for an attack. And from that suggestion, Washington devised another plan that many thought was utterly impossible. But a young, aggressive, energetic member of the team named Colonel Henry Knox didn't think so. Knox was a bookseller before the war and had almost no military experience. But when Washington asked him to travel to Fort Ticonderoga in New York and retrieve the stockade's artillery inventory, Knox made the impossible happen in short order. Across the mountains, in the dead of winter, through deep snow, Henry Knox hauled fifty-nine guns back to Cambridge. And then, while American troops were diverting the redcoats' attention with artillery fire from the north, General Washington moved the cannon by night to Dorchester Heights overlooking Boston to the south.

More than 2,000 men worked all night employing hundreds of oxcarts to carry the guns, ammunition, and building materials to the Heights. Once there, they dug trenches, erected barricades, and set the artillery in place. The work began at dusk and finished at dawn.

Soldiers present later commented that the brightness of the

full moon that night allowed them to see what they were doing. It also allowed them to view the silhouette of a tall man on a horse—riding back and forth all night long, issuing orders, providing direction, and encouraging the men in their work. On this cold, critical night, General George Washington did not sleep in his warm, comfortable tent. He was on the mountain with his troops.

The next morning, five additional regiments joined those already on Dorchester Heights. And when the British awoke and gazed to the south, they were terrified by what they saw. One British engineer described the overnight emplacement of artillery as an "astonishing" feat—and considered that the work "must have employed from 15,000 to 20,000 men."

That morning (March 5), the fifth anniversary of the Boston Massacre, George Washington addressed the men manning the guns on Dorchester Heights. He fully expected the British to attack his position and, in fact, they were planning an immediate assault with nearly half their forces. A witness recorded Washington's remarks.

> General Washington said to those who were at hand: "Remember it is the fifth of March, and avenge the death of your brethren!" It was immediately asked what the General said by those that were not near enough to hear, and as soon answered; and so from one to another through all the troops, which added fresh fuel to the fire. . . .

Before the British could carry out their plan, however, a violent, sustained thunderstorm struck the area and prevented the attack. The British then reconsidered their action and decided to wait and observe. Then, several days after the rains let up, Washington, sensing the British were in a defensive posture, ordered a massive military movement of several regiments toward the channel separating Dorchester from Boston. The maneuver was interpreted by the British as prelude to an all-out attack. Washington wrote that the next morning the streets of Boston were full of "great movements and confusion amongst the troops the night and day . . . in hurrying down their cannon, artillery, and other stores to the wharves with the utmost precipitation." The redcoats were dumping their larger artillery into the water; sails were hoisted on nearly all British ships at the Boston docks; and about 1,200 Tories were desperately attempting to buy space so as not to be left behind. "The hurry in which they have embarked is inconceivable," said the awestruck Washington.

On March 17, 1776, the entire British force evacuated Boston by sea. When Washington's men swarmed into the city they found dummies propped up as sentinels holding defective muskets.

General George Washington, in command of an undisciplined, untrained, ragtag army of Americans, had achieved one of his country's goals without firing a shot. He had intimidated, outmaneuvered, and outfoxed the enemy. As a result, after several long years of British occupation, Boston was again back in American hands—and free.

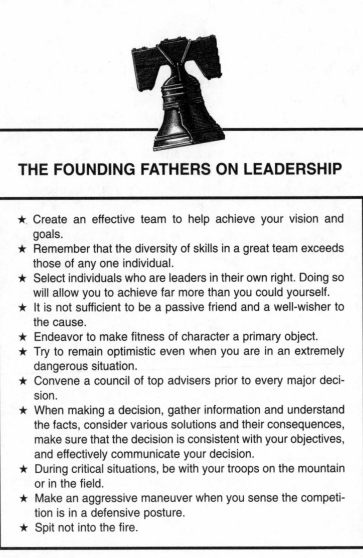

THE FOUNDING FATHERS ON LEADERSHIP

★ Create an effective team to help achieve your vision and goals.

★ Remember that the diversity of skills in a great team exceeds those of any one individual.

★ Select individuals who are leaders in their own right. Doing so will allow you to achieve far more than you could yourself.

★ It is not sufficient to be a passive friend and a well-wisher to the cause.

★ Endeavor to make fitness of character a primary object.

★ Try to remain optimistic even when you are in an extremely dangerous situation.

★ Convene a council of top advisers prior to every major decision.

★ When making a decision, gather information and understand the facts, consider various solutions and their consequences, make sure that the decision is consistent with your objectives, and effectively communicate your decision.

★ During critical situations, be with your troops on the mountain or in the field.

★ Make an aggressive maneuver when you sense the competition is in a defensive posture.

★ Spit not into the fire.

"O ye that love mankind! Ye that dare to oppose not only the tyranny but the tyrant, stand forth! Every spot of the old world is overrun with oppression. Freedom hath been hunted around the globe. O! Receive the fugitive, and prepare in time an asylum for mankind!"

Thomas Paine,
Common Sense,
January 10, 1776

"We hold these truths to be self-evident: that all men are created equal; that they are endowed by their Creator with certain inalienable rights; that among these are life, liberty, and the pursuit of happiness."

Thomas Jefferson,
The Declaration of
Independence,
July 4, 1776

4 / *Inspire the Masses*

TEAM LEADERS
Thomas Paine
Thomas Jefferson

As 1775 gave way to 1776, the Second Continental Congress vacillated between seeking a complete separation (advocated by the radicals) and stepping up diplomatic efforts aimed at reconciliation (preferred by conservatives). Because each of the thirteen colonies had separate and distinct governments, none had officially directed their delegates to pursue independence. Groups loyal to the Crown assembled, became more vocal, and appealed to Parliament for support. With each bloody encounter, more moderates swung toward the call for independence. Eventually, though, things came to a complete political gridlock. What was viewed as patriotism by one group was termed treason by the other.

As a result, the future was obscure in the minds of the vast majority of American citizens. Most seemed to prefer a return to circumstances as they existed prior to the Sugar Act of 1764. Many common folk in rural areas wondered what all the fighting was about. And as more and more questions arose as to why America should wage war with Great Britain, it became apparent that there were no compelling answers, no organized communications effort to justify such drastic action.

It is not an uncommon occurrence for events to come to a standstill when an organization is on the brink of a major change. In America's situation, there was not a single individual who could have ordered or dictated a movement toward independence. People on both sides felt equally strong-minded as to the justice of their cause. If a revolution was going to take place, a great majority of people had to be the catalyst, spurring their representatives on to take appropriate action.

Several of the founding fathers clearly understood the key leadership principle of inspiring others rather than coercing them—and that the word "inspiration" includes an element of emotion that propels people to take action on their own initiative. As a group, the founding fathers turned to the members of their team who had skills and expertise to do more than simply persuade a few individuals of the need for independence from Great Britain. They turned to those who had the potential to motivate great masses of people in a relatively brief period of time.

At this juncture, the man stepping forward to assume the mantle of leadership was an obscure, penniless writer who had failed at nearly every job he had ever tried. And, irony of all ironies, he was a common Englishman who had first set foot on American soil in November 1774. His name was Thomas Paine.

In England, Paine had attempted to earn a living as a corset maker, a Methodist preacher, a grocer, an excise officer, an English teacher, and a writer. Even though he was a poor businessman and had trouble relating to others, Paine was an imaginative and creative literary genius. His special gift showed itself at a relatively young age when, as a teenager, he devoured books of all kinds—even those written in Latin. As a young man, he was known for his impetuosity, for his dynamic energy and risk-oriented nature, and for the piercing genius in his eyes.

While in London, Paine caught the attention of Benjamin Franklin, and when he made it known that it was his intention to set sail for America, Franklin recommended Philadelphia and offered a letter of introduction. Upon arrival, Paine landed a job as a staff writer with a new periodical called *The Pennsylvania Magazine*. He not only penned numerous articles for his new employer, he became involved in a loosely organized campaign of literature in defense of liberty—writing poems, essays, and other stories.

After returning to Pennsylvania in 1775, Ben Franklin, along with Dr. Benjamin Rush, another leading radical patriot (who would later became surgeon general of the Continental Army), suggested that Paine write an independence-oriented pamphlet. And, inspired by their confidence in him, Paine set out on a mission to compose a great story. He was also propelled to action by his own innate sense of right and wrong. "When the country into which I had just set my foot was set on fire about my ears," he said, "it was time to stir."

By September, Paine had finished a first draft and read it aloud to Dr. Rush, who praised the manuscript and offered a number of suggestions for improvement. As it was simple and easily understood, he suggested that it ought to be entitled *Common Sense*. In early December, Paine sent the new draft to Franklin and Sam Adams for final review and revisions. And on January 10, 1776, the work was published in the form of a cheap mass distribution pamphlet (at a cost of two shillings each).

Adams, Franklin, and Rush all knew that the timing was perfect for an informative and inspiring pamphlet. However, the thirty-nine-year-old Paine was totally unprepared for what would happen next: The first edition of *Common Sense* sold out in less than two weeks in Philadelphia; within three months, it had sold more than 120,000 copies throughout the colonies; and, over the next two years, it would sell more than half a million around the world. Further, it was quickly translated into French and Polish—and distributed all over Europe.

One would think that the author of such a successful work would instantly become famous and wealthy. However, not only was the pamphlet published anonymously, Thomas Paine quietly donated all his royalties to the Second Continental Congress to do with as they saw fit. He did not take a cent for his work.

In *Common Sense*, Thomas Paine challenged the existing paradigm that the offspring American colonies needed the protection of Mother England, that the elaborate government of a monarchy/parliament was more effective than simple local governments, and that the American economy would better prosper under the umbrella of the great economic power of England. Paine argued that Americans had been influenced by "ancient prejudices and . . . superstition." He stated that the colonies did not need the mother country's protection; that the simpler the government the better; that "government, even in its best state, is but a necessary evil; in its worst state, an intolerable one"; and that because of all the oppressive acts, the American economy actually *suffered* under the strong arm of England.

With stirring and audacious rhetoric, Thomas Paine was taking a great risk. In essence, he well knew that he was committing an act of treason. That is one reason why the pamphlet was published anonymously at first. As a matter of fact, many people conjectured that it had been written by Franklin or Adams—largely because few outside of Philadelphia had even heard of the true author.

Paine's intellectual argument in the pamphlet was striking because, in part, he was not intimidated at all by the power of the Crown. He aggressively attacked not only British authority itself (George III was the "Royal Brute of Britain"), but also every argument he had ever heard against American independence. In addition, Paine's points were remarkably cogent and original, filled with imagination and creativity. Essentially, he analyzed the situation from a childlike point of view, with no past biases. He started from scratch, with a clean slate. In doing so, he created an opportunity for everyone who read his pamphlet to gain a clear view of all the arguments underlying a move toward independence.

Throughout *Common Sense*, Thomas Paine's tone was emotional, indignant, angry, and challenging. At the same time, the writing was eloquent. He offered only "simple facts, plain arguments, and common sense." Average farmers, as well as the most renowned statesmen of the day, understood his writing. Paine strategically realized that only through plain talk could the great masses of people be mobilized toward a single line of thinking. In the prologue to *Common Sense*, for instance, he wrote: "As it is my design to make those that can scarcely read understand, I shall therefore avoid every literary ornament and put it in language as plain as the alphabet."

Moreover, part of Tom Paine's literary genius lies in the reality that his writing was crafted for the spoken word as well as the written word. That he intended his work to be read both in private and out loud is evident in his statement: "I bring reason to your *ears*, and, in language as plain as A, B, C, hold up truth to your *eyes*" [italics added]. As a matter of record, *Common Sense* was frequently read out loud to people who could not read.

Thomas Paine clearly possessed a number of attributes

common to what Howard Gardner (in *Leading Minds*) termed an "exemplary" leader. Such a leader, he noted, is "an effective communicator . . . [with] the capacity and the inclination to use words well." Gardner also wrote that "leaders attempt to convince others of a . . . clear vision of life"; that "stories are the most powerful weapon in the leader's literary arsenal"; and that "the less sophisticated story remains entrenched.

"The rarest individual," wrote Gardner, "is the leader who creates a new story"; and that a childlike approach can be "strikingly imaginative," and exhibit "a willingness to entertain new possibilities, and an openness to unfamiliar practices that . . . older individuals are well advised to try to maintain."

In *Common Sense*, Thomas Paine openly advocated a new and original political thought. "Power of the people" had really never been seriously considered in Europe. It was his argument that monarchies and parliaments ultimately had no control over the great masses of people unless they gave their approval and support; and that groups of citizens acting together to achieve common goals could, in fact, render a king powerless. "Tis not in numbers," wrote Paine, "but in unity that our great strength lies; yet our present numbers are sufficient to repel the force of all the world."

He also placed the current situation in a broad historical context. "The present time . . . is that peculiar time that never comes to a nation but once," he wrote. "The sun never shined on a cause of greater worth. . . . Posterity will be affected by the proceedings now. . . . We have it in our power to begin the world over again."

And then Paine did what is simply innate to all great leaders—he issued an eloquent call to action. "Everything that is right or reasonable pleads for separation," he advocated. "The blood of the slain, the weeping voice of nature cries, 'TIS TIME TO PART.' . . . O ye that love mankind! Ye that dare to oppose not only the tyranny but the tyrant, stand forth! Every spot of the old world is overrun with oppression. Freedom hath been hunted around the globe. O! Receive the fugitive, and prepare in time an asylum for mankind!"

Common Sense exploded onto the American scene with a deafening blast. It was read aloud on city streets, passed around in schools and clubs, and preached from the pulpits of churches. It spawned spirited public debates nearly everywhere because, as John Adams noted, it offended almost as many people as it inspired." "It burst from the press," wrote Benjamin Rush, "with an effect which has rarely been produced by types and papers in any age or country." Benjamin Franklin called the impact of the pamphlet "prodigious." And George Washington, who had *Common Sense* read aloud to the troops, stated that it had "sound doctrine and unanswerable reasoning," and that it was "working a powerful change in the minds of many men."

Paine's pamphlet was either read or heard by almost every American citizen—and patriots everywhere began to take action with spirit and fearlessness. People in Pennsylvania began a series of moves to toss out loyalists who dominated the state legislature—and then sent representatives to Congress who supported independence. Connecticut merchants and businessmen openly violated the Crown's trading restrictions and navigation acts. Virginia tobacco farmers refused payment of their debts to British creditors. And after returning from the Continental Congress in Philadelphia, Colonel Christopher Gadsden burst into South Carolina's provincial congress carrying a copy of *Common Sense* in one hand and, in the other, a handmade yellow flag bearing the inscription: "DON'T TREAD ON ME." He immediately advocated "absolute independence for America," and, shortly thereafter, South Carolina acted on Henry Laurens's motion to declare a temporary constitution, in effect declaring its own independence from Great Britain.

Common Sense caused a decisive and spontaneous change in thought and action all across America. People were now thinking what was previously unthinkable. The word first whispered by John Adams to members of Congress—"independence"—was now shouted across the land. "Nothing else is now talked of," said one Bostonian, "and I know not what can be done by Great Britain to prevent it."

Paine had provided an opportunity for the general public to view their current situation through an unclouded lens, from a different angle, in a new and different way. As a result, he was able to reverse the previously existing assumptions that mired people in their existing paradigm. Such a reversal is a critical foundation for every successful transformation or revolution. Moreover, Thomas Paine achieved this reversal with pure leadership—by inspiration rather than coercion. He tapped into people's hopes and longing aspirations—and brought them to the surface with significant emotional impact. In short, as the definition of leadership reads, he *inspired others to act—for certain shared goals that represent the wants and needs, the aspirations and expectations—of the people.* Clearly, this one man, with the encouragement of others, had touched off an unstoppable movement that would result in the American colonies declaring their freedom from Great Britain.

When *Common Sense* was first released, the Continental Congress watched and waited for the reaction of the people at large. As their wishes became clear, radical delegates began acting quickly, and conservatives (many of whom had been swayed by Paine's compelling arguments) were forced to respond to public opinion. Representatives like Dr. Benjamin Rush now had a mandate to move.

On May 15, Congress recommended that the individual colonies sever all relations with Great Britain and create new and independent governments "as shall best conduce to the happiness and safety of their constituents in particular, and America in general." This resolution was introduced by none other than John Adams, who had first proposed the idea back in 1774 only to see his motion tabled. But Adams had not dropped his goal. And when Paine opened the door of opportunity, Adams immediately walked through it. Eventually, all the colonies not only declared their independence from the Crown, they convened conventions and adopted individual constitutions—thereby making each an independent state.

On June 7, 1776, Richard Henry Lee of Virginia rose in the Second Continental Congress and introduced a resolution with three primary elements: 1) formulation of a new continental constitution, 2) establishment of foreign commercial alliances, and 3) a declaration of independence. The delegates knew that if they were to gain their independence from Great Britain, the thirteen colonies would have to act together—hence the need for an overarching constitution of some sort. They also knew there was no chance to win a war against England without the support of other nations (which was one of the goals earlier established by John Adams). And, finally, all the members knew that there was little hope of attaining foreign alliances as long as their situation was perceived as a family squabble. Therefore, a formal declaration of independence was not only desired, but required.

Four days later, on June 11, Congress established a committee of five to draft the document. The appointed members were: Benjamin Franklin, John Adams, Roger Sherman of Connecticut, Robert Livingston of New York, and Thomas Jefferson. Congress then agreed to a three-week moratorium on the independence issue until the committee could get back to them.

When the committee first met, the other members asked Jefferson to take on the job of writing the declaration. Not only was he a respected intellectual and known for his writing skill, there were certain political reasons for assigning Jefferson the task. Members from the New England states wanted to gain the support of the middle colonies (who thought well of Jefferson). By contrast, John Adams was mistrusted and viewed in some circles as a fanatic. And to the southern states Jefferson was, of course, very popular.

When Adams asked Jefferson to take the lead, he gave three reasons: "Reason first, you are a Virginian, and a Virginian ought to appear at the head of this business. Reason second, I am obnoxious, suspected and unpopular. You are very much otherwise. Reason third, you can write ten times better than I can."

"Well," responded Jefferson, "if you are decided, I will do as well as I can."

The humility and self-knowledge displayed by John Adams paved the way for the creation of one of the most compelling documents in history. What's more, it would be written by a thirty-three-year-old man who was content to let others take the lead and had, for the most part, labored diligently in the background to that point. Now it was his turn to step forward.

Thomas Jefferson was much more than simply a writer. He was a statesman, philosopher, architect, scientist, inventor, and musician. Many who knew him well felt he was also a genius of the highest caliber. He loved reading about nearly all subjects and, during his lifetime, amassed a library of thousands of books. He had grown up in Albemarle County, Virginia, in a bright, church-oriented family. While Thomas was close to his mother, he also adored his father and looked to him as a role model. The elder Jefferson's death, occurring when Tom was only fourteen years old, devastated the boy.

Jefferson went on to study law at the College of William and Mary, passed the bar in Virginia, and set about to practice of law. In 1772, he married a young widow, Martha Skelton, from Williamsburg. Together they had six children, only two of whom survived childhood. Over the next ten years, he would experience the trauma of several deaths in his immediate family. In 1774, his second infant daughter died; in 1776, just a few months before he was to write the Declaration of Independence, his mother died unexpectedly—giving him a migraine headache that lasted six weeks; and in 1782, his wife died. Jefferson never married again.

In a remarkable political career, Thomas Jefferson was elected to the Virginia House of Burgesses at the age of twenty-six. Even then, he was known as a visionary thinker by his contemporaries. He immediately identified with and fell into the group of radicals associated with Patrick Henry. As such, Jefferson became totally dedicated to the cause of independence. He vowed that he "would go to hell to serve his country" and he swore "eternal hostility against every form of tyranny over the mind of man."

In 1774, after Virginia's governor dissolved the state assembly, Jefferson was elected to the First Continental Congress. Although he did not attend due to his wife's illness, he sent along *A Summary View of the Rights of British America*, which advocated a natural right to self-government for America. The document made Jefferson quite well known and as John Adams remarked, "gave him a reputation for literature, science, and a talent for composition." Upon being elected to the Second Continental Congress in 1775, Jefferson drafted the "Declaration of the Causes and Necessities of Taking Up Arms." By all accounts, Thomas Jefferson was a modest man, spoke little while Congress was in session, and performed his work behind the scenes.

Jefferson took two weeks to draft the Declaration of Independence. He did not base his document on any previous work and, indeed, did not even consult other books or pamphlets. All the words and organization came directly from his mind and, as a result, it turned out to be an original literary masterpiece.

Franklin and Adams reviewed Jefferson's first draft, made a few minor revisions, but it was presented to the entire Congress largely untouched. When the first of July rolled around, Richard Henry Lee's motion for independence was considered. The unofficial vote count showed only nine states in favor. The South Carolina, Delaware, and Pennsylvania delegations were divided. New York's representatives did not have guidance from their home legislature, so they would not vote.

John Adams quickly became the Declaration's most ardent advocate and he provided a powerful voice. "Before God, I believe the hour has come," declared Adams in debate. "My judgment approves this measure, and my whole heart is in it. All that I have, and all that I am, and all that I hope in this life, I am now ready here to stake upon it. Live or die, survive or perish, I am for the Declaration. Independence now, and independence forever."

While Adams was taking the lead in an attempt to persuade the doubting states, other radicals who found themselves in a minority sprinted into action. For instance, Caesar Rodney, Delaware's pro-independence delegate, rode all night to Dover and back in an effort to gather information and persuade his colleagues to vote yes. Even Thomas Paine was lurking around the halls of Congress during the breaks as he persistently nagged and pestered delegates to vote for independence. As a matter of fact, during the three-week moratorium, Paine made it his personal mission to be a lobbyist in favor of the Declaration—however it might read in final form.

But the event that really turned the tide in favor of the resolution was relayed by a dispatch from George Washington. The general reported that a British fleet of more than a hundred vessels had sailed into New York Bay and were preparing to land on Staten Island in what seemed to be preliminary to an all-out attack on American positions.

That did it.

South Carolina's delegates immediately changed their minds—knowing full well that Charleston, which had already fended off the British once, might be next. Two of Pennsylvania's conservatives left the room and one decided to vote yes. And Delaware's representatives, thanks in part to Rodney's all-night ride, voted in favor. As a result, on July 2, Congress approved Richard Henry Lee's motion for independence. Then Congress turned to the Declaration itself.

The delegates revised Jefferson's draft primarily by deleting certain words and phrases. However, all realized the document was sound—well-structured, eloquent, piercing—and the representatives, by and large, knew that they could not improve it much. Each change, however, was like a knife in Jefferson's body. He could almost not bear it, but was comforted largely by Benjamin Franklin's encouragement and delightful sense of humor. The only thing Jefferson never got over was the deletion of the sentences concerning the word "slavery." The delegates from South Carolina and Georgia demanded the change and it is doubtful the Declaration would have had any impact had not the southern colonies been in complete support. Jefferson relented and on July 4, 1776, the Second Continental Congress officially approved the Declaration of Independence—thereby giving birth to a new nation.

Thomas Jefferson stated in later years that his intent was "to place before mankind the common sense of the subject, in terms so plain and firm as to command their assent and to justify ourselves in the independent stand we are compelled to take. [The Declaration]," he said, "was intended to be an expression of the American mind."

The political purpose of the Declaration was not only to declare independence but to justify a separation from Great Britain. Jefferson stated as much in the opening paragraph:

> When in the course of human events, it becomes necessary for one people to dissolve the political bands, which have connected them with another, and to assume among the powers of the earth, the separate and equal station to which the laws of nature and of nature's God entitle them, a decent respect to the opinions of mankind requires that they should declare the causes which impel them to the separation.

The Declaration was specifically aimed at King George III, largely because the colonies had already disclaimed Parliament's authority. The power of the Crown over the colonies was the final tie with Great Britain in need of repudiation. The document, in fact, did not mention Parliament at all. "[The king] has combined with others to subject us to a jurisdiction foreign to our construction," it read, "and unacknowledged by our laws; giving his assent to their acts of pretended legislation."

In concise, crisp prose, with rhythm and structure, Thomas Jefferson outlined the essence of grievances the American colonies had against England. He employed remarkable creativity and imagination and a lofty eloquence that tended to raise the reader's spirits. Moreover, Jefferson's words elevated the entire cause of independence to a higher level than it had ever before been. Now, the American Revolution was not just about overcoming a tyrant and gaining independence—it was a struggle for the natural rights of man, for self-government, for freedom itself for all humankind for all time:

> We hold these truths to be self-evident, that all men are created equal; that they are endowed by their Creator with certain inalienable rights; that among these are life, liberty, and the pursuit of happiness; that to secure these rights, governments are instituted among men, deriving their just powers from the consent of the governed.

While Jefferson's words were eloquent and inspiring to most people, they tended to alarm conservative members of Congress. Clearly, the Declaration stated that people possessed something of an innate right to rise up and overthrow *any* government that did not secure those "self-evident" rights. "Whenever any form of government becomes destructive . . . ," read the Declaration, "it is the right of the people to alter or to abolish it, and to institute new government. . . ." In 1776, such a notion was not only new, it was almost audacious. No one, other than Thomas Paine, had ever had the courage to place it at the forefront of political thought—let alone stand up and declare it valid for the whole world to hear.

But Thomas Jefferson's confidence in the document and in his own beliefs never wavered during the course of his lifetime. He wrote the Declaration to stand the test of time.

On July 8, the Declaration of Independence was read in public for the first time in Philadelphia. And throughout the summer, there were public readings in every major city in every major colony. It was published in newspapers, copied, reprinted, and widely disseminated throughout the colonies. Spontaneous celebrations took place all across the country in honor of America declaring its independence. Church bells rang all day, guns were fired, and parades were held. Members of the Sons of Liberty in Bowling Green, New York, even toppled a lead statue of King George III and shipped most of it off to Connecticut where it was melted down and molded into thousands of bullets.

People now had a common cause. The Declaration of Independence became a point around which everyone could rally. It inspired in others a serious reason for action—and it literally drew everyone into the war.

But similar to *Common Sense*, the Declaration of Independence was an act of treason against the government of Great Britain. And, without a doubt, Jefferson and all the other delegates to the Second Continental Congress knew it. It was for this reason that the names of the signers of the declaration were not made public for another six months.

John Hancock, president of the Congress, was the first to sign the Declaration. And he might have been thinking back to 1768 when the British had filed criminal charges against him, because, as he said, he signed in large letters so that King George III "might read it without his spectacles." In all, fifty-six delegates signed during the summer of 1776. The youngest was Edward Rutledge (twenty-six) of South Carolina; the eldest, at seventy years, was Benjamin Franklin. All but eight were born in America, and most were wealthy or prosperous.

"We must be unanimous," said Hancock to the others on July 4. "There must be no pulling different ways. We must all hang together."

"Yes," replied Benjamin Franklin, "we must indeed all hang together, or most assuredly we shall all hang separately."

The founding fathers knew there would now be no turning back. It was all or nothing. The last line in Jefferson's document stated their dedication: "For the support of this Declaration . . . we mutually pledge to each other our Lives, our Fortunes, and our sacred Honor."

But the Declaration of Independence, while of paramount importance, was only a step in their leadership journey. They had sounded the trumpet to let people know there was a problem. They had created a vision, set goals, and become organized. They had taken decisive action and built a superb team. And they had succeeded in inspiring the great masses of people to get behind them and act. The founding fathers had prepared well for the Revolution. Now it was time to fight the war.

THE FOUNDING FATHERS ON LEADERSHIP

★ Inspiration includes an element of emotion that propels people to take action on their own initiative.

★ Encourage others to take the lead.

★ Analyze your situation with a childlike point of view, with no past biases.

★ Only through plain talk can the great masses of people be mobilized toward a single line of thinking.

★ Craft your writing for the spoken as well as the written word.

★ Remember, the less-sophisticated story remains entrenched.

★ Issue an eloquent call to action.

★ A reversal of assumptions that mire people in their existing paradigm is critical to every major transformation.

★ Communicate in terms so plain and firm as to justify yourself in the stand you are compelled to take.

★ Elevate your cause to a higher level—one that will inspire people.

★ Read all major communications to the troops.

★ Rally every member of the organization to a common cause.

PART II
MOBILIZING AND MOTIVATING

"I never heard either of them speak ten minutes at a time, nor to any but the main point. . . . They laid their shoulders to the great points, knowing that the little ones would follow of themselves."

Thomas Jefferson,
on George Washington
and Benjamin Franklin

"These are the times that try men's souls. The summer soldier and the sunshine patriot will, in this crisis, shrink from the service of his country; but he that stands it now, deserves the love and thanks of man and woman."

Thomas Paine,
The American Crisis,
December 19, 1776

5 / *First Listen, Then Communicate*

TEAM LEADERS
George Washington
Thomas Paine

On July 9, 1776, George Washington received a copy of the Declaration of Independence along with a personal note from John Hancock. After reading the document carefully, he immediately issued a general order:

The Continental Congress . . . [has declared] the United Colonies of North America free and independent states: The brigades are to be drawn up at

six o'clock, when the Declaration of Congress is to
be read with an audible voice.

The General hopes that this important event
will serve as a fresh incentive to every officer and
soldier to act with fidelity and courage, as knowing that now the peace and safety of his country
depends (under God) solely on [our] success.

That evening the soldiers of the Continental Army and
local militias stood spellbound as the Declaration was read
aloud. Afterward, the men broke into spontaneous cheers
and applause with (as Washington wrote) "expressions and
behavior of both officers and men testifying their [ap-
proval]."

Great leaders, whether they are guiding a country or a
corporation, always ensure that followers are informed and
educated on current events related to the organization's effort. They communicate their messages with simplicity, consistency, and clarity. In this particular instance, George
Washington did not hesitate in his decision. For him, communicating the Declaration to the troops was a natural thing
to do—similar to the time he had Paine's *Common Sense*
read aloud. After all, America declaring its independence was
a major event; and the soldiers needed to receive such basic
information not only because they were a crucial part of the
team, but because the document itself was a motivating and
inspiring force.

Accordingly, Washington had the Declaration read aloud
almost at once—so people could hear it together and discuss
it together. Moreover, it was a direct communication—read
in total, without filters or editing. Nor did the general make
any specific modifying comments of approval or disapproval.
He let people interpret its meaning for themselves.

Disseminating information and rallying others through
timely communication was one of the very first strategies
employed by the founding fathers. It was done, in part, out

of simple necessity. Because of the great distance from England, major communications were often delayed by weeks or months—as were those between the colonies themselves because the American territory was vast and sparsely settled. As such, people in urban communities were considerably more informed than were those in rural areas, remote from hubs of shipping markets and commerce.

Interestingly enough, the formation of the Continental Army helped to bridge some of the communication gaps. The army brought people from distant regions together. Those who thought of themselves as Pennsylvanians or Virginians began to view each other collectively as Americans. And as soldiers went home on leave, they would spread news of interesting events and tell their stories in the most remote regions of the land.

The founding fathers also sent out flyers and handbills, wrote propagandist literature in the form of pamphlets and newspaper articles, and employed slogans and such symbols as liberty trees, liberty poles, liberty caps, and liberty bells. Further, in July 1775, a committee in Congress recommended the creation of a system ensuring rapid transmission of information throughout the colonies. As a result, Congress established a post office department with Benjamin Franklin as postmaster general. The Continental Congress also regularly dispatched two- or three-man committees to visit General Washington and see for themselves the status of the army's operations. Washington, in turn, frequently journeyed from the field to Philadelphia (or wherever Congress might be) to confer with congressional representatives. His visits lasted from a few days up to two weeks depending on the agenda and the time of year (winter inactivity usually allowed more time to be away).

Proper communication was key to George Washington's success—both in building personal relationships and in fighting the war. As a matter of fact, a primary element in his military strategy revolved around both disseminating and re-

ceiving timely information. For instance, he persistently attempted to disrupt British communications by cutting their
lines of communication and by misleading the redcoats as to
his own intentions. "Much trouble was taken and finesse
used," Washington wrote in his diary, "to misguide and be-
wilder [the British], in regard to the real object, by fictitious
communications as well as by making a deceptive provision
of ovens, forage and boats in [their] neighborhood."

And in regard to releasing specific information about his
plans and maneuvers, Washington often kept his own troops
in the dark until the very last minute: "Nor were less pains
taken to deceive our own army," he wrote, "for I had always
[believed], when the deception does not completely take
place at home, it would never sufficiently succeed." In the
long haul, the Continental Army became so effective at
spreading disinformation that the British were constantly
suspicious of all tips relating to American maneuvers.

General Washington also developed a rather elaborate intelligence and counterintelligence system that included spies
and espionage. He and Nathanael Greene jointly chose
Major John Clark, an aide to General Greene, to serve as
"chief of spies." It was his assignment to create a wide network of agents and operatives whose purpose was to gather
reliable detailed information about British troop activities—
and to disperse false information about American operations. Major Clark collected all the information and then
forwarded it directly to Washington, who assumed personal
responsibility for determining which data to act upon or ignore.

While the commander in chief was willing to pay a significant fee to American spies, there were few funds budgeted
for such a purpose. However, as it turned out, large amounts
of money were not needed. Most of the people who joined
the network did not care about getting paid. They were
proud to help—to do their part in the fight for freedom.

One of the most famous spies of the American Revolution

was Nathan Hale—a twenty-four-year-old, Yale-educated schoolteacher and poet from Connecticut. During the fall of 1776, in an attempt to gather information on enemy troop movements, Hale had slipped behind the British lines in New York. He was captured on September 21 and taken to General William Howe, commander of British forces. With only his Yale diploma for identification, and papers outlining his mission, Hale confessed that he was indeed a spy for George Washington. As such, Howe summarily ordered him hanged the next morning. Several British officers and regulars reported being impressed with the courageous and proud manner in which the young man went to the gallows. One redcoat recorded that, when asked if he had any last words, Nathan Hale said: "I regret that I have but one life to lose for my country."

George Washington reacted quietly to the news of Hale's death. He is said to have been moved by the courage and sacrifice of the young patriot, and he would remember the event in the future when days were dark.

Washington, by nature, was not a gregarious talker. He was, for the most part, a quiet gentleman. A frequent reader of the controversial literature of the day, he constantly sought out such authors as Thomas Paine, James Madison, Alexander Hamilton, and Thomas Jefferson. It was Jefferson who once commented of both Washington and Benjamin Franklin that he "never heard either of them speak ten minutes at a time, nor to any but the main point. . . . They laid their shoulders to the great points, knowing that the little ones would follow of themselves."

Part of George Washington's leadership style was to listen first, then communicate his feelings. While such a technique may sound like common sense, it can be argued that history is filled with stories of failed leaders who acted without asking—or who took decisive action without first verifying key information. Washington, however, was most often deliberate and pragmatic. Recall that his first action upon arriving in Boston was to ride out on his horse and get the lay of the land—and ask for an accurate count on the number of troops (both American and British). Afterward, he convened a council of war and listened to the opinions of his generals. It was only then that he conceived and executed a plan of action. In general, Washington employed the same method before every major engagement of the war. He sought out key information, attempted to verify it, and then took swift action.

A mistake common to many executives is not taking time to listen to others. Many think that because they are chosen to head up a group they are, in turn, responsible for coming up with every idea, making every decision, and instituting every action. Such leaders often feel that if they aren't doing it all, they will be viewed as ineffective. However, it is the leader who doesn't mingle and obtain comments from others who is the one that has the most difficulty getting things done. Nobody knows how to do the job better than those on the front lines. So frequent contact with followers is essential if leaders are going to succeed.

Listening is not only an important aspect of leadership, it is also an art. Like a painter in touch with his subject, effective listeners take in everything they hear, analyze it within the context of the environment, and then create an image for their minds to absorb. Stephen R. Covey, in *Principle-Centered Leadership,* wrote that leaders "listen to others with genuine empathy," and that they "seek first to understand, then to be understood." In essence, leaders simply must be good listeners. How else can they understand and act for *"certain goals that represent the values—the wants and needs, the aspirations and expectations—of the people they represent"?*

Leaders must listen to people in their organizations far more than followers must listen to leaders. They must listen, then speak; follow, then lead. Of course, such a concept is anything but new. More than 2,000 years ago, the ancient Chinese philosopher Lao Tzu wrote in the Tao Teh Ching:

> In [the leader's] desire to be at the front of
> people,
> He must in his person be behind them.
> In his desire to be above the people,
> He must in his speech be below them.
> Sincere words are not showy;
> Showy words are not sincere.
> Those who know do not say;
> Those who say do not know.

After the British abandoned Boston and their ships disappeared over the horizon, George Washington ordered his entire army on an overland march to New York City. Arriving in the city on April 13, 1776, he joined up with General Charles Lee, who had already begun to build fortifications. Working together, the two devised a strategy to defend the city. They knew that it would be impossible to prevent British ships from entering the bay and they guessed that the obvious landing place would be on Staten Island, six miles south of Manhattan. As a result, it was decided to concentrate troops in New Jersey, on Long Island, and on the northern edge of the city. Whether or not they could hold New York depended on how large a force the British sent.

Washington had, indeed, been correct in his assumption. The grand strategy of British forces was to occupy and divide the entire state of New York so as to sever New England from the other states. And they would start with New York City because of its obvious importance to American economic activity. On July 3, the day after Congress voted for independence, General William Howe landed 9,300 troops on Staten Island. Nine days later, a British fleet carrying another 11,000 troops arrived off the coast of New York City to join him.

Panic reigned in the streets as word spread that two royal frigates had sailed up the Hudson to Tappan Zee unopposed by the American artillery that was put in place to prevent just such an occurrence. And terror struck in the hearts of New Yorkers as they watched ship after ship sail into New York Bay. One contemporary account described the sight:

> Onlookers gazed with awe on a pageant such as America had never seen before—five hundred dark hulls, forests of masts, a network of spas and ropes and a gay display of flying pennants. There were ships of the line with frowning sides, three-tiers of guns and high forecastles; there were graceful frigates, alert and speedy, tenders and galleys to land the thousands of men from the unwieldy transports.

General Washington immediately issued orders that all men were to keep their guns with them at all times and be ready for action at a moment's notice. By August 1, however, it was clear that the Americans would not be able to hold their ground. On that date, another forty ships, with an additional 2,500 land troops aboard, arrived in New York carrying General Henry Clinton and Lord Charles Cornwallis. Shortly thereafter, more than 8,000 Hessian mercenaries also landed. As a result, by mid-August, the British had amassed more than 30,000 troops in what was the largest expeditionary force they had ever deployed overseas—not to mention the overwhelming size of the British navy that had sailed into New York's waters.

Overwhelmingly outnumbered, the Americans were pushed back. On August 29, after valiant fighting on Long Island at the battle of Brooklyn Heights, the army suffered more than 1,000 casualties. Unable to achieve any sort of victory, and hoping to avoid total annihilation, Washington engineered a massive retreat to Manhattan. Two weeks later, at the battle of Kip's Bay (presently 34th Street and the East River), the Americans suffered another catastrophic loss and retreated all the way to Harlem Heights, a high land area between the Harlem and Hudson rivers some twelve miles to the north. In doing so, they completely abandoned New York City, losing artillery, supplies, and hundreds of men.

Within a week, the city of New York burned—a result of deliberate arson by local American reactionaries. Area newspapers noted that "the fires raged with inconceivable violence, and in its destructive progress swept away all the buildings [and houses] between Broad Street and North River," and that "many hundreds of families are destitute of shelter, food, and clothing." A good amount of British military supplies was also destroyed in the process.

The last quarter of the year has sometimes been referred to as the "dark days of 1776"—largely because the British military forces began to rattle off an impressive string of victories over the ill-equipped Americans. On October 12, Fort Ticonderoga fell to the British. On October 28, the city of White Plains was taken. On November 16, Fort Washington, on the New York side of the Hudson River, was overwhelmed by the British and, four days later, Fort Lee (on the New Jersey side) had to be abandoned.

By December 1, the terms of enlistment for soldiers from New Jersey and Maryland had expired, and the army's ranks began to thin dramatically. Unable to hold his positions, General Washington was forced to withdraw and retreat. Within a week, the Continental Army was completely on the run—fleeing across New Jersey for dear life. In mid-December, General Charles Lee was captured at Morristown and Washington himself had barely made a successful retreat to the west bank of the Delaware River.

News reached Philadelphia that a rout was on, and members of the Continental Congress began to panic. When it was confirmed that British General Howe was near Trenton, New Jersey—just a hop, skip, and jump from Philadelphia—

the entire Congress fled to Baltimore to avoid capture. Soon thereafter, they passed a general resolution that essentially gave George Washington dictatorial command over the colonies.

As the entire weight of the American Revolution fell on General Washington's shoulders he was faced with a seemingly insurmountable task. The government was not only on the run, it was facing a potentially catastrophic financial crisis. The union itself was, at best, shaky. And to top it all off, casualties, expired enlistments, and desertions had decimated the ranks of the Continental Army. There were now only 3,500 American troops remaining from the original 20,000 Washington had started with. Of those who had stayed, morale was extremely low—and with good reason. In a matter of months, they had lost nearly the entire state of New York and had not a single victory to their credit. The situation looked bleak, indeed.

There were, however, two overriding factors that rescued the American cause in these dark days of 1776. First, George Washington did not concede that defeat was imminent. Rather, he remained optimistic, positive, and actually began thinking about an offensive. The other element that helped turn the tide involved Thomas Paine, who had once again felt impelled to step forward and act.

After Congress declared independence, Paine had joined a group of Pennsylvania volunteers called a "flying camp." Similar to short-term task forces in modern corporate America, the flying camps of the American Revolution were comprised of volunteers who enlisted for a brief term of duty and then "flew" into an ongoing battle zone. When the conflict concluded, the flying camp disbanded.

It just so happens that Paine's group immediately marched to Amboy, New Jersey—located off the tip of Staten Island, New York, where the British began their invasion. They arrived just a few days before the first 9,300 redcoats landed and stayed for two months until the fighting moved north. Paine then headed up to Fort Lee where General Nathanael Greene appointed him as one of his aides.

For the most part, Tom Paine served as a field correspondent writing eyewitness battle accounts for the Philadelphia press. His style of writing proved to be new and different—providing readers with a compelling, detailed account of events shortly after they occurred. He was there when Fort Washington was surrounded and taken by Lord Cornwallis. As a matter of fact, Paine had stood with General Greene on the other side of the Hudson River watching helplessly as the entire encampment of 2,000 men was forced to surrender. And when many of the troops inside Fort Lee subsequently became frightened and began to desert, Paine tried to rally them, in part, by passing out copies of *Common Sense*.

But only a few days later, more than 6,000 redcoats and Hessians attacked Fort Lee and forced Greene's troops to abandon the fort and hightail it through the back country of New Jersey. Thomas Paine was there and saw more and more deserters run off. He saw men whose enlistments had run out leave in droves. And he was there when Washington crossed the Delaware leaving the British on the other side—snarling, shouting, and angry that the general had been shrewd enough to take all the boats with him.

During that distressing month-long retreat from Fort Lee to Trenton, Paine wrote another essay. By day, he ran with the troops; but by night, he sat next to the campfire, using a drumhead as a desk, scribbling down his thoughts. Shortly after reaching Trenton, Paine took off for a thirty-five-mile trek to Philadelphia where he hoped to publish his new work. He walked alone—the entire way—with only his notes and a few scraps of food for sustenance. When he arrived in Philadelphia, the editor of *The Pennsylvania Journal* read his manuscript and agreed to publish it immediately: 18,000 copies in the form of an eight-page pamphlet. Thomas Paine entitled it *The American Crisis*.

George Washington was among the first to receive copies. After reading it himself, the general once again called groups of his demoralized troops together and had Paine's new essay read aloud. It began:

> These are the times that try men's souls. The summer soldier and the sunshine patriot will, in this crisis, shrink from the service of his country; but he that stands it now, deserves the love and thanks of man and woman. Tyranny, like hell, is not easily conquered; yet we have this consolation with us, that the harder the conflict, the more glorious the triumph. What we obtain too cheap, we esteem too lightly: 'Tis dearness only that gives everything its value. Heaven knows how to put a proper price upon its goods; and it would be strange indeed if so celestial an article as Freedom should not be highly rated.

Paine went on to commend the army's "orderly retreat for nearly a hundred miles." And then vowed that the American cause would either be won through "perseverance and fortitude," or lost through "cowardice and submission."

The American Crisis had a major positive effect on the morale of the troops. They were instantly uplifted, given new hope, and motivated to stay with the Continental Army. And as the pamphlet circulated widely, many members of the militia and army, who had either deserted or fled after their terms of enlistment had expired, headed back to the front. As a result, Washington's forces slowly built back up to fighting strength. Overall morale took a decided turn for the better. Courage returned to the troops. And private citizens pitched in and helped with supplies and support. In short order, the tide turned—if only in people's minds.

During a time of great despair, when there was nothing being communicated but fear and rumors, when, as the writer said himself, "our affairs were at their lowest ebb and things in the most gloomy state," Thomas Paine had almost single-handedly renewed the spirit of American independence. And, what's more, he was anything but finished with his work. *The American Crisis*, in a series of thirteen separate essays released at critical times, would have a life of its own throughout the rest of the American Revolution. Paine had taken it upon himself to help ensure effective communications that would keep the organization informed and inspired.

Thomas Paine had been with the troops. He had listened to their fears and their concerns, their hopes and their dreams. Then he began to think. After he thought, he began to write. And the message he communicated inspired people to renew themselves, to rise to a greater level of awareness, and, ultimately, to a higher level of achievement. Just like George Washington, the general—Thomas Paine, the literary genius, the artist—had listened first, and then communicated his feelings.

During the fighting in New York, when the Americans were on the run, British Admiral Richard Howe sent a captured American general (John Sullivan) to Philadelphia to request a private meeting. Howe believed that, given his overwhelming force and the outcome of the recent battles, the Americans might be willing to negotiate a surrender. Congress, in turn, delegated the task to Benjamin Franklin, John Adams, and Edward Rutledge—who hastily set out for Staten Island where the meeting was to be held.

When the delegates reached New Brunswick, New Jersey, where they had planned to spend the night, they found the local inn filled to near-capacity. Franklin and Adams agreed to share a small room with only one bed and a tiny window. When Franklin entered the room, he threw open the window. But shortly before retiring, Adams closed it—and

Franklin immediately reacted. "Don't shut the window," he bellowed. "We'll be suffocated."

"I do not wish to catch cold," protested the younger Adams.

"Come, come," said the seventy-year-old, "I don't believe you're acquainted with my theory of colds. Open the window and I will convince you that I'm correct."

That ended the argument. Benjamin Franklin had successfully appealed to John Adams's innate curiosity. As a result, an intrigued Adams opened the window and listened to the old man speak about his theory of colds.

When the American delegation reached Staten Island the next day, they were cordially escorted in to meet with Admiral Richard Howe. Lord George Germain, the British secretary of state for the colonies, was also present and recorded the substance of the meeting:

> The three gentlemen were very explicit in their opinions that the associated colonies would not accede to any peace or alliance, but as free and independent states; and they endeavored to prove that Great Britain would derive more extensive and more durable advantages from such an alliance, than from the connection it was the object of the commission to restore. Their arguments not meriting serious attention, the conversation ended, and the gentlemen returned to Amboy.

And so it went. Even in a time of great discouragement, the founding fathers did not abandon the people's wishes to be free. On the contrary, given the opportunity to speak directly to British authority, they audaciously attempted to persuade the British that they were wrong and the Americans were right. The entire episode, however, turned out to be a futile attempt at diplomacy for both sides—and, as a redcoat enlisted man was to remark shortly afterward: "They met, they talked, they parted—and now nothing remains but to fight it out."

Also in the fall of 1776, during those dark days, a resolution in Congress created a new name for the American colonies. Henceforth, the country would be called "The United States of America."

THE FOUNDING FATHERS ON LEADERSHIP

★ Communicate your messages with simplicity, consistency, and clarity.

★ Communicate in total, without filters or editing. Provide a forum where people can hear the message together and discuss it together.

★ Bringing people together from distant regions helps to bridge gaps in communication.

★ A primary element in your overall strategy should involve disseminating and receiving timely information.

★ Be a frequent reader of the controversial literature of the day.

★ You do not need to speak for more than ten minutes at a time, nor to any but the main point.

★ Do not act without asking. Take time to verify key information.

★ Listen, then speak; follow, then lead.

★ When things look darkest, stay optimistic and positive; plan an offensive.

★ Create "flying camps" in your organization.

★ Work by day, think by night.

★ Remember that one inspiring communication can turn the tide.

"To form a just idea, it would be necessary to be on the spot."

> George Washington,
> at Valley Forge, Pennsylvania,
> February 16, 1778

"If I see any man turn his back today, I will shoot him through. I have two pistols loaded. But I will not ask any man to go further than I do. I will fight as long as I have a leg or an arm."

> George Washington,
> to the troops just before the
> battle of Long Island,
> August 1776

6 / Travel with the Troops

TEAM LEADER
George Washington

During much of the Revolution, as time and military situation permitted, General Washington invited all officers on field duty to dine with him at 3:00 each afternoon. Such meetings were, of course, more frequent between battles and during winter months. The officers craved time with their leader—and Washington both liked and needed to spend time with them.

These gatherings created enjoyable opportunities for immediate and continuous communication. The individuals involved got to know one another better, aired their differences, learned their similarities, and, as a result, built trust, respect, and confidence among themselves. As the top leader, Washington was able to size up the abilities of his people; what their strengths were; their skills; their weaknesses. It also allowed him to convey values, ideas, and general information related to the effort in which they were all engaged. The officers, in turn, were given opportunities to be part of the planning process—to advise and consent.

The fact that he was able to hold daily meetings with his officers is a lesson in and of itself, as it reveals a cornerstone of George Washington's natural leadership style—which was, simply, to travel with the troops. He was, quite literally, always in the field with his soldiers. More than two centuries later, in modern corporate America, the very same strategy would be dubbed MBWA (Managing by Wandering Around) by Tom Peters and Robert J. Waterman in their book, *In Search of Excellence.* The concept has also been referred to as "roving leadership," "being in touch," or "getting out of the ivory tower." Whatever the label, it is simply the process of stepping out and interacting with people, of establishing *human contact.*

Washington wasn't the first, nor would he be the last great leader to make a habit of personal interaction with followers. During the Civil War, Abraham Lincoln frequently visited the troops in neighboring states—and General Ulysses Grant maintained that he would not rent "a house at the capital and direct the war from an armchair in [the city]." Franklin Roosevelt, even though he was confined to a wheelchair, kept a crowded schedule of meetings and interviews at the White House. Frequently, his wife, Eleanor, traveled in the president's place—proudly noting that she was "my husband's legs." And Harry Truman was famous for his "whistle-stop" campaign and regular evening walks.

In the practice of leadership, such two-way communication has a tendency to create and strengthen emotional bonds that set the stage for ongoing positive relations. By interacting widely, leaders provide members of the organization a welcome chance to have a say in how things are done. And by simply showing respect and admiration for others, leaders enhance their own credibility.

During the years of the Revolution, Washington felt he had no other option than to lead by example. Ultimately, the fate of the entire nation rested in his hands—and he knew it. His assignment involved organizing, training, and inspiring inexperienced and undisciplined troops in an effort to achieve America's freedom and independence. The situation could not possibly have been handled from some distant office. "To form a just idea," Washington said at Valley Forge, "it would be necessary to be on the spot." And George Washington was there—"on the spot"—for virtually the entire eight-year duration of the American Revolution. During one six-year stretch, he did not return to his home in Virginia at all. Also, in the last forty-five years of his life, he spent nearly twenty of them away from Mount Vernon in the service of his country.

Upon assuming command of the Continental Army, Washington instilled rigid discipline in the troops. He drilled the men constantly—keeping them out of trouble by keeping them busy. In the beginning, as a matter of fact, the general was relentless. In 1775, when he arrived in Boston and heard a full accounting of the battle of Breed's Hill, Washington court-martialed half a dozen men for cowardice. "I never spared one [officer] that was accused of cowardice but brought them to immediate trial," he noted a full year before the British landed in New York. So it was small wonder that when Washington, just before the fighting began north of Staten Island, threatened to punish anyone who deserted their posts, the men had no doubts he meant exactly what he said.

When the British sailed up off the coast of New York in August of 1776, they dispatched an officer ashore with a flag of truce to meet with the Americans. Washington, in turn, sent three officers of his own to cordially confer with the redcoats on the beach. The British offered a full pardon and guaranteed protection to any Americans who would lay down their arms and swear allegiance to the Crown. But Washington categorically refused to negotiate on any terms.

Immediately thereafter, the arrogant and overconfident British began their amphibious landing of troops. There seemed to be no respect for the army of the colonies. Indeed, the entire mission appeared not to be taken very seriously by the majority of men arriving. "With the disembarkation of about 15,000 upon a fine beach, their forming upon the adjacent plain," one witness recorded, "the soldiers and sailors seemed as merry as in a holiday."

A few days later, at 1:00 A.M. on the morning of August 27, 1776, George Washington, in Manhattan, was trying to catch some shut-eye when he awoke to cannonfire on Long Island. He immediately ordered reinforcements to be sent in that direction and jumped into a boat to get over there. When he arrived, the American troops were nervously gathered, ready to take on thousands of British redcoats and German mercenaries (Hessians).

The general quickly mounted a horse and rode along the lines of troops—persistently encouraging the men and reminding them what they were fighting for. "The hour is fast approaching," he said, "on which the honor and success of this army and the safety of our bleeding country depend. Remember, officers and soldiers, that you are freemen, fighting for the blessings of liberty—that slavery will be your portion, and that of your posterity, if you do not acquit yourselves like men. . . . The fate of unknown millions will now depend, under God, on the courage and conduct of this army."

In his exhortations, Washington linked their fighting to a greater cause, and tried to provide his soldiers with a broader understanding of what they were really fighting for. He also attempted to motivate them with a little fear. "Will you resign your parents, wives, children and friends to be the wretched vassals of a proud, insulting foe?" he asked them. "And your own necks to the halter?"

And then, just before the enemy attacked, Washington

shouted out to his men: "Let them approach within twenty yards before you fire." And, drawing his pistols, he turned to some youthful soldiers and said: "If I see any man turn his back today, I will shoot him through. I have two pistols loaded. But I will not ask any man to go further than I do. I will fight as long as I have a leg or an arm."

As expected, the British forces attacked the American right flank where General Washington was positioned. In a few minutes, though, they also launched a surprise attack on the left, and the Hessians charged up the center. Under heavy enemy fire himself, Washington could not stop General John Sullivan's men from being overrun in the center, or General William Alexander's troops from suffering the same fate on the left. As a result, by noon, Sullivan, Alexander, and more than 1,000 men had been captured. "Good God," a soldier heard Washington exclaim, "what brave fellows I must this day lose!"

At the very moment when things looked bleakest for the American forces, they received some unexpected help from none other than the British commander, General William Howe. Surveying the situation from a nearby hill, Howe issued an order to halt the offensive. "Enough has been done for one day," he said. Many of the British officers and men protested—citing that they could gain a crushing victory if they kept on the offensive. But the commander had made up his mind and kept repeating his order until all activity was finally halted.

The next day it began to rain fiercely as a Nor'easter storm rolled into the area—thereby preventing the British from launching an attack or even an artillery bombardment. But as Washington surveyed the situation he found his men "dispirited" and, as he later wrote Congress, "to be almost broke down." Many of the American soldiers wandered aimlessly about. Or they stood soaked in their trenches, some in waist-deep water. Gunpowder got so wet it became unusable, and most men did not have bayonets.

Later that evening, Washington called his executive officers together for a council of war. They unanimously agreed that their current situation was untenable. What was left of the main American army, some 8,000 troops, were trapped on an island with the possibility of being completely sealed off by the British fleet when the weather cleared. Faced with the realization that his risky strategy of concentrating almost his entire force on Long Island had backfired, General Washington made a desperate decision. It was now apparent they had to get out while the getting was good. So he ordered a massive retreat across the East River.

As soon as darkness fell, every rowboat and fishing boat was gathered—and the entire 8,000-man American army began ferrying themselves across more than a mile of water—all night long—in a continuous rain. Washington himself headed down to the river to personally supervise the whole operation. He ordered the men to stoke their campfires and keep them burning as long as possible, and to move quietly and in an orderly fashion. When the morning sun began to rise over the hills, and hundreds of men had still not crossed over, an unexpected fog settled in and became so thick that boats could not be seen more than six feet from shore. Fortunately, neither could enemy lookouts see anything of the American activity.

When the fog began to lift, General Washington finally got on a boat—one of the last to do so. He and the men with him were the only troops fired upon as the British could finally see what was going on. Shortly after reaching the other shore, Washington penned a letter to Congress notifying them of the events of the previous six days. He apologized for not communicating earlier but, as he explained, he had been "quite unfit to write or dictate till this morning. I had hardly been off my horse and had never closed my eyes."

When informed that Washington had effectively disappeared with his entire army, British General Howe was incredulous. In this daring, unprecedented, and totally unexpected move, George Washington had narrowly avoided a catastrophe. He had fought and run away. But the Continental Army remained intact—and would survive to fight another day.

Over the next two weeks, American troops entrenched themselves on the coast of Manhattan and waited for another British attack. Meanwhile, Washington sent out snipers into the woods, and small patrols to harass the British any way they could.

This time, General Howe's next moves were more deliberate and aggressive. He had been embarrassed by Washington's unorthodox escape and wished to put an end to the thing once and for all. His plan called for a distracting artillery bombardment of the center and right flanks of American positions while landing a massive force on Washington's left flank at Kip's Bay, which was also bombarded.

On Sunday morning, September 15, while eighty flat-bottomed boats loaded with 4,000 British and Hessians shoved off from Long Island (presently Astoria), half a dozen royal frigates opened fire on the American positions. The artillery bombardment at Kip's Bay, coupled with thousands of troops landing in front of them, terrified the Americans. They threw down their guns, leaped from their trenches, and tripped over each other as they ran blindly to the rear. Officers, also frightened, quickly gave the order to retreat without waiting for their commander in chief's approval.

Meanwhile, Washington, who had stationed himself at Harlem Heights (about five miles away), had heard the sound of the guns and was riding up the Post Road at a full gallop toward Kip's Bay. When he got there, he rode smack into thousands of his men fleeing for their lives in the opposite direction. "Stop," he ordered. "Take the walls, take the cornfield." But the troops completely ignored him and kept running.

Washington then lost his temper. He pulled out one of his

pistols and fired it into the air, he began striking some of the soldiers with his riding crop while calling them "dastardly sons of cowardice," and then he pulled his saber and threatened to run through the next man he encountered. Finally, in total frustration, Washington threw his hat to the ground and cried: "Good God, have I got such troops as these? Are these the men with whom I am to defend America?" In his subsequent letter to Congress, he stated that he had "found the troops retreating . . . flying in every direction, and in the greatest confusion. I used every means in my power to rally and to get them into some order; but my attempts were fruitless."

At last, all the American troops passed him by, and Washington was left sitting on Old Nelson, his beautiful white mount, all by himself, in despair. As the front line of British troops approached and began shooting, Washington just turned and looked at them. Nathanael Greene later said that he felt the general would rather die than live at that point. Then two aides rode into the fray, grabbed Old Nelson's reins, and led their commander in chief away to safety. At that point, the British and Hessian troops stopped firing and actually cheered George Washington's bravery. They had never before seen anything like it.

Washington, who had not received so much as a scratch, then calmly sent a rider back to the main city with orders for the rest of the army to retreat and regroup at Harlem Heights (today the north side of Central Park). After two more councils of war, Washington and his generals agreed to abandon New York City altogether and head north toward Forts Washington and Lee. "It is now extremely obvious, from all intelligence," he wrote Congress, "that having landed their whole Army. . . they mean to enclose us on the Island of New York by taking post in our rear. Having therefore their system unfolded to us, it became an important consideration [in our decision]."

Had George Washington not been on the spot with his troops during the battle of Brooklyn Heights/Long Island, the entire American army would have been captured and the war would have been over before it had begun. And while Washington could not stop his frightened troops from retreating at Kip's Bay, it did not deter him from later riding to the sound of the guns—again and again—until the troops, one day, would finally hold their ground and turn defeat into victory.

Leading by example, just as George Washington did during the American Revolution, has the effect of both motivating and mobilizing others in a common cause. Achieving results is directly proportional to a leader's willingness and ability to interact with people in the field. Research shows that the more frequent the human contact, the more results will be achieved. It's merely common sense that leaders cannot be effective unless they have the consent of those who would follow them.

In general, there are five major reasons for employing a strategy of frequent human contact in leadership:

1. Obtain information and make timely decisions.

The best leaders realize that obtaining accurate and instant information is key to making quick, effective decisions. As Winston Churchill once said: "As a general rule, the most successful man in life is the man who has the best information." Leaders need to be right there in the field where they can see things for themselves and act quickly in response to developing events.

2. *Understand what people think and feel.*

If leaders perpetually seek personal contact with people, they will then know exactly what others think and how they feel. Therein lies the most fundamental of all leadership principles, which ties back to the definition of leadership: *Leaders act for the wants and needs, the aspirations and expectations—of the people they represent.*

3. *Keep people informed.*

Frequent contact with others allows the leader to keep people informed about the direction of the organization, what's being achieved on other fronts, and how it may affect the current work of the individual. The adage "Knowledge is power" is never more appropriate than in the relationship between leader and followers.

4. *Obtain feedback.*

Dialogue with others allows leaders to receive feedback on both personal performance and ideas they have presented. This not only keeps the leader on track with the desires of the people, but also aids in the refinement and improvement of new initiatives. Moreover, it fulfills the basic human needs for personal growth and the comfort that comes with knowledge that one's actions are appreciated. Being open and receptive to new ideas—as well as criticism—is an important trait for a leader to possess.

5. Inspire and innovate.

Being in the field allows leaders to quickly size up a situation and implement new ideas (conjured up from both leaders and followers) that arise in response to specific events. It also provides many opportunities to inspire people by reminding them what they are fighting for, by charging into action, or by elevating the cause to a higher plane.

On the morning of November 15, 1776, George Washington was at Fort Washington surveying the situation and speaking with the soldiers and officers who would have to defend their garrison in the face of a fast-approaching enemy force. That afternoon, he rejoined the main army in New Jersey where he conferred with General Nathanael Greene. But the very next day, British General William Howe approached Fort Washington and demanded an unconditional surrender. Although outnumbered three to one, the officer in charge, Colonel Robert Magaw, flatly refused to surrender, stating that Americans were involved in "the most glorious cause that mankind ever fought in."

Shortly thereafter, as Washington and Greene were rowing across the Hudson River to consult with Magaw about evacuation, the British began their attack—forcing the two generals to return to Fort Lee. The redcoat and German troops subsequently leveled a crushing defeat on the Americans—capturing Fort Washington, all its supplies and munitions, and taking 2,858 American prisoners of war. General Howe then ordered Lord Cornwallis to take 6,000 men into New Jersey and chase down the rest of the American forces. It was at this point that the Continental Army was in full retreat and thousands of men fled as their enlistments expired.

All along the way General Washington was sending out false information that he was preparing to stop and take a stand. But he never did. By the time the Americans reached Trenton, New Jersey, on December 3, their British pursuers were tired and frustrated. "They will neither fight nor totally run away," complained a redcoat officer. "They keep at such a distance that we are always above a day's march from them. We seem to be playing Bo-Peep."

THE FOUNDING FATHERS ON LEADERSHIP

★ Hold regular, informal gatherings that provide enjoyable opportunities for immediate and continuous personal communications.

★ Remember that two-way communication has a tendency to
create and strengthen emotional bonds.

★ To form a just idea, you must be on the spot.

★ Keep people out of trouble by keeping them busy.

★ Link your mission to a greater cause. Provide people with a
broader understanding of what they are really fighting for.

★ Lead by example.

★ When in a desperate situation, head down to the river and
personally supervise the entire operation.

★ Retreat when you must. Live to fight another day.

★ During periods of relative inactivity, harass.

★ Ride to the sound of the guns.

★ The more frequent the human contact, the more progress will
be achieved.

★ When outnumbered, keep at a distance. Neither fight nor totally run away.

"It is fearfully cold and raw and a snow storm setting in. The wind is northeast and beats in the faces of the men. It will be a terrible night for the soldiers who have no shoes. Some of them have old rags tied around their feet, but I have not heard a man complain."

George Washington,
prior to crossing the Delaware,
December 25, 1776

"The dejection lasts only for a moment; they soon rise out of it with additional vigor; the glow of hope, courage and fortitude will, in a little time . . . kindle the whole heart into heroism."

Thomas Paine,
The American Crisis No. IV,
a day after the American loss at
Brandywine Creek, Pennsylvania,
September 12, 1777

"You might have tracked the army from White Marsh to Valley Forge by the blood of their feet."

George Washington, 1778

7 / *Turn a Negative into a Positive*

TEAM LEADERS
George Washington
Thomas Paine

On December 8, 1776, George Washington ferried what was left of his military force across the Delaware River into

Pennsylvania. The last of the troops disappeared across the water just as the first of the redcoats arrived on the scene. However, the British could not follow anytime soon because Washington, thinking ahead, had taken with him all boats within fifty miles.

The American army had dwindled to less than 5,000 soldiers, many of whom were exhausted, starved, and sick; and nearly all were without adequate clothing or supplies. But, once again, overconfident British commanders were not inclined to press for an attack. After all, winter was setting in, the Americans were in bad shape, and it appeared that the rebellion had all but collapsed. So just before Christmas, Washington received intelligence that General William Howe had withdrawn to New York and suspended military operations for the winter. In the meantime, he had left a garrison of Hessians in Trenton under the command of Colonel Johann Rahl, who was informed by his superiors that the Americans "have not three hundred men" and were "almost naked, dying of cold, without blankets, and very ill-supplied with provisions."

Meanwhile George Washington never seriously considered resting on his laurels, but, rather, was concerned that so many enlistments were due to expire on January 1 that he would be left with only 1,200 regulars. He is said to have asked one of his officers what the consequences would be if his army were to retreat even further. When the reply came that the entire state of Pennsylvania surely would be lost, Washington grabbed his throat and responded: "My neck does not feel as though it was made for a halter." And after being told that Germans were known to "make a great deal of Christmas," and that the Hessians occupying Trenton would probably celebrate well into the night with heavy drinking, General Washington decided to recross the river and launch a daring surprise attack.

By mid-afternoon on Christmas Day, 2,400 Americans were marching nine miles upriver to McKonkey's Ferry—all along the way staying behind low hills so as not to be seen by British sentries. In an effort to inspire his men, Washington circulated copies of Thomas Paine's *The American Crisis*, and passed on the countersign "victory or death" for the impending battle. At 6:00 P.M., the general recorded in his diary: "It is fearfully cold and raw and a snow storm setting in. The wind is northeast and beats in the faces of the men. It will be a terrible night for the soldiers who have no shoes. Some of them have old rags tied around their feet, but I have not heard a man complain."

Washington crossed the Delaware—with soldiers, horses, and artillery—at night, under cover of darkness, in freezing cold weather, during a storm mixed with snow, rain, and hail. The entire crossing took nearly nine hours. By the time everyone had reached the other side at 4:00 A.M., their clothing was wet or frozen and much of their gunpowder was soaked through. When the order was given for the march south to Trenton, two of the many soldiers who had lain down to rest in the snow were found dead.

During the march, the men were asked to be as quiet as possible—and orders were relayed through a chain of whispered commands. As the troops slogged through ice and snow, some left a trail of blood from their exposed or bare feet. Two regiments were sent north to block the road to Princeton should the enemy attempt to retreat in that direction. And just prior to the attack (which occurred shortly after dawn), General Washington passed out an order: "Soldiers, keep by your officers," he advised. "For God's sake, keep by your officers!"

When the Americans descended on Trenton, the Hessians were taken completely by surprise. Many poured out of their quarters into the streets hungover and clad only in their nightshirts. And because Washington had attacked with a driving wind at his back, the enemy had to contend with snow and sleet blowing directly into their faces. Then, as the Hessians attempted to assemble, an order was given to artillery captain Alexander Hamilton to fire cannons at point-blank range.

Colonel Rahl, who had been drinking heavily at the Trenton Tavern the night before, died from wounds inflicted by the artillery barrage.

Within two hours, the battle was over. In addition to taking 1,000 prisoners, the Americans had also captured artillery, ammunition, forty horses, about 1,000 muskets, and other supplies (including food and clothing). By contrast, Washington's troops had suffered only four slightly wounded men during the battle. One of those was a young officer named James Monroe—who would later become the fifth president of the United States.

After briefly convening his top officers for a council of war, Washington decided to take all prisoners and supplies back to Pennsylvania. So in short order, the entire American force marched back up to McKonkey's Ferry and hauled everyone and everything back across the Delaware River to safety.

George Washington had succeeded in lulling the British into a false sense of security. They had tired of the American commander's "Bo-Peep" tactics and also grew overconfident that the outmanned and unclothed Americans were no match for their superior forces. As such, the British leaders had absolutely no reason to suspect that the American commander would be so audacious as to risk his entire army in an attack on Trenton. Moreover, George Washington had, once again, asked the impossible of his troops—to march all night, in desperately cold weather, without sleep—and then engage the enemy in battle. Even more remarkable, they responded to him and won an improbable victory.

Washington's triumph at Trenton breathed new life into the American cause. It was the first really positive occurrence in a long line of negative events. Trenton turned what had seemed to be imminent total defeat into an inspiring win. All leaders may learn a lesson from George Washington's action in recrossing the Delaware. Rather than looking at things from the conventional viewpoint—or thinking a situation is hopeless—leaders should watch for an opportunity. It's when the competition pulls back, when they believe you're down for the count, that leaders have a great opportunity to strike and achieve a major triumph.

After the victory, morale and enthusiasm naturally increased among the troops. Washington, himself, took quick advantage of the opportunity. He offered every man who would reenlist for six weeks a bounty of ten dollars. And he personally made an emotional appeal to his men: "My brave fellows," he said upon assembling the troops, "you have done all I asked you to do, and more than could be reasonably expected, but your country is at stake: your wives, your houses, and all that you hold dear. If you will consent to stay . . . you will render that service to the cause of liberty and to your country which you probably never can do under any other circumstances." After Washington spoke, somewhere between 1,000 and 1,400 men reenlisted.

On the second of January, 1777, British General Cornwallis, bivouacked at Princeton, arrived in Trenton with the main portion of an 8,000-man force. His goal was to take out the American army once and for all—and reverse the momentum Washington had created. Arriving in the afternoon, Cornwallis was advised by his officers to attack immediately—as the bulk of the Americans were vulnerably grouped next to Assunpink Creek, a tributary of the Delaware. But the British general rejected their advice and commented that he'd "bag the fox" the next morning. Several subordinates protested their superior's decision. "Washington won't be there in the morning," the officers told Cornwallis.

They were right. This time, however, the American commander did not intend to retreat; he planned another daring night maneuver—first going around the left flank of the British, and then heading ten miles north to attack the British garrison at Princeton.

The march began at 1:00 A.M.—while most of the enemy was sleeping. Artillery caisson wheels were wrapped in rags to muffle the sound as they rolled over ice and snow; no soldier under the rank of general was allowed to know anything about where they were headed; and the Americans traveled on a newly constructed trail, the Quaker Road, of which the enemy was not aware. Washington also ordered 400 men to stay behind and deceive the British sentries into thinking they were preparing for a major defense by noisily digging trenches and stoking campfires. Then, at dawn, they were to slip out and head north to rejoin the rest of the troops.

At first light, British lookouts near Princeton spotted the lead American troops headed by General Hugh Mercer, and rushed out in force to meet them. When the redcoats opened fire, the general's horse was shot out from under him—and then the British began a wild bayonet charge. As Mercer pulled out his sword to fight back, he was overpowered and stabbed to death. When the American troops saw their leader go down, they broke and ran. As some terrified men threw down their weapons and tried to surrender they were also stabbed and killed.

General Washington, located a short distance away with the next regiment, swiftly rode in the direction of the shots. Upon encountering the retreating troops, he shouted out to them to stand their ground. Waving his hat furiously, Washington then rode past the Americans to within thirty yards of the British advancing forces. At that point, a redcoat volley sounded and smoke filled the air, hiding Washington from view. One American officer thought he saw the general's horse rear back and fall. But when the smoke cleared, Washington was still standing tall on his white steed. Unscathed, he began motioning for his men to turn around and attack. "Bring up your troops, my dear Colonel," he shouted to Colonel Edward Fitzgerald. "This day is our own." When the retreating troops saw their commander risk his life in such a courageous manner, they turned and followed him with such fierceness that, this time, the British troops broke and ran in the other direction—abandoning Princeton in the process.

The Americans not only won another thrilling victory, they had also captured the entire supply depot for Cornwallis's 8,000-man force. Washington then loaded the provisions on wagons and began to withdraw his men to the north. Meanwhile, after the British troops at Trenton had awoken to find the Americans missing, they immediately hastened back to Princeton. Upon reaching the outskirts of the town, they were forced to walk through chest-deep water because Washington had blown up the bridge over Stony Brook. When Cornwallis's army finally did march into Princeton, he was just in time to see the American rear guard leaving in the distance. After letting his men dry out and rest, the British commander then headed north to New Brunswick in hopes of protecting the supplies he had stashed there. Surely, thought Cornwallis, that was where Washington was taking his army.

But he was mistaken. The American commander had decided it was time to move into winter quarters. He chose Morristown, New Jersey, which was centrally located forty miles north of Trenton and twenty-five miles west of New York. A small town nestled in the Watchung Mountains and not easily accessible, it provided a strategic site that allowed Washington to keep an eye on the main British army (now snug and warm in New York City). By the time the Continental Army reached Morristown, nearly the entire state of New Jersey was free of a British-occupied threat. It had taken Washington only two weeks to accomplish the task. And when he finally decided to rest his troops, it was in a place that was less than a day's ride from the main contingent of British forces.

On March 12, Congress returned to Philadelphia from their refuge in Baltimore. Within a month, John Adams nominated Thomas Paine to be secretary of the Committee for Foreign Affairs (previously called the Committee of Secret Correspondence). Adams had cited the fact that Paine "was poor and destitute," and that "we might put [him] into some

employment where he might be useful and earn a living."
Meanwhile, Paine had published two more installments of *The
American Crisis* in his ongoing effort to inspire others to sup-
port the American cause.

Paine's actions, along with Washington's exhilarating victories at Trenton and Princeton, began to work some magic as
the Continental Army, having fought off a bout of smallpox
at Morristown, began to regroup and rebuild. By early spring,
their numbers again exceeded 8,000.

It was a good thing, too, because at that point the British
had begun their grand strategy of dividing the northern states
from the southern ones. In April, they defeated local American forces at Norwalk and Ridgefield, Connecticut, and
burned Danbury to the ground. In May, British General John
Burgoyne landed his army in Quebec and started a march
south to take Fort Ticonderoga (which fell on July 5).

By mid-July, General William Howe set sail with 260 ships
and more than 18,000 British troops and disappeared into the
Atlantic. General Washington, uneasy with this development,
ordered four divisions to march immediately to Philadelphia
just in case that was Howe's destination. More than a month
later, he received word from scouts that the British fleet was
sighted entering the Chesapeake Bay. Howe had decided to
take the safer, and slower, circuitous route to Philadelphia.
Washington then quickly moved the rest of the Continental
Army to New Castle (fifty-five miles south of Philadelphia),
where the British forces would have to disembark. Once
there, Alexander Hamilton pushed for an all-out attack. "I
would not only fight them," he said, "I would attack them—
for I hold it an established maxim that there is three to one in
favor of the party attacking."

Traveling on the road to Philadelphia, the two armies con-
verged at Brandywine Creek on September 11. The British,
with superior numbers, outflanked the Americans when
Cornwallis and 7,500 redcoats (nearly the entire size of the
Continental Army) marched in a circuitous seventy-five-mile

route to come up from behind. General Washington, facing General Howe's 10,000-plus contingent in his front, was taken completely by surprise and immediately ordered a full retreat. Hours of heavy fighting ensued and only nightfall prevented the complete annihilation of the American army. General Cornwallis then decided to rest his troops rather than pursue the enemy in darkness.

When word reached Thomas Paine in Philadelphia that Washington's army had suffered casualties of more than 1,000 dead and over 400 wounded, he worked furiously through the night on a fourth installment of *The American Crisis* and had it published the next day. In this four-page pamphlet, he wrote:

> Those who expect to reap the blessings of Freedom must, like men, undergo the fatigue of supporting it. It is not a few acres of ground, but a cause that we are defending. . . . It is natural for men to feel concern [at such a circumstance]. But the dejection lasts only for a moment; they soon rise out of it with additional vigor; the glow of hope, courage and fortitude, will, in a little time . . . kindle the whole heart into heroism.

At the end of the essay, Paine directly addressed General William Howe: "We fight, not to enslave, but to set a country free, and to make room upon the earth for honest men to live in. We are sure we are right," he told the British leader, "[and that you are] the tool of a miserable tyrant."

Thomas Paine's words served to inspire Americans only temporarily. And even though Congress immediately requested reinforcements from Maryland, New Jersey, New York, and Pennsylvania, there seemed to be no way of stopping the overwhelming British force.

As Howe marched steadily toward Philadelphia, General Washington constantly changed his position so as not to be outflanked again. Part of the American strategy was to harass the enemy as much as possible until an advantageous position could be achieved. With that idea in mind, Washington dispatched 1,500 men under the command of General Anthony Wayne to Paoli, Pennsylvania, with a mission to disrupt the British baggage train and rear guard. Local Tory sympathizers, however, tipped off the redcoats to Wayne's presence and, on September 21, General Charles "No-Flint" Grey (so-called because he had his men remove the flints from their muskets) led a surprise British bayonet attack late at night. The Americans suffered hundreds of casualties—many of whom were killed as they slept.

The Paoli massacre shook George Washington to the core, terrified the residents of Philadelphia, and energized the British forces in their determined trek to the capital of the colonies. A few days later, church bells tolled all around Philadelphia signaling the enemy's approach. While Congress disbanded again and fled (this time to York), the Pennsylvania state legislature took off for Lancaster. And within hours, nearly 10,000 residents (one third of the population) had left town—running for their lives.

Thomas Paine, however, stayed. He packed his personal belongings and private papers in a trunk and shipped it out of town on a boat. He waited until just shortly before General Cornwallis paraded six divisions (four British, two Hessian) into Philadelphia with bands playing and English loyalists cheering. Then Paine headed for the Continental Army and stayed with the troops.

After about a week, Washington and his generals decided to attack the main British force stationed at Germantown, only five miles from Philadelphia. Once again, they planned a surprise attack—sneaking up on the redcoats at night. However, when a thick fog rolled in at the start of the battle, the American troops became confused and disoriented. A staggering loss resulted, with the Continentals suffering 700 casualties compared to the redcoats' 534.

The following morning, Thomas Paine had breakfast with George Washington and attempted to lift the general's spirits. "Even though the expedition failed," Paine told the commander in chief, "it had some good effect [in that] the men seemed to feel themselves more important after it than before, as it was the first general attack they had ever made." Washington appreciated Paine's kind words, but subsequently moved his exhausted troops to the vicinity of White Marsh, Pennsylvania, to reassemble.

Over the next six months, Thomas Paine stayed in the field—following the American military campaign and reporting on its progress. After Germantown, he rejoined General Nathanael Greene as an aide-de-camp, and was crossing the Delaware headed to Fort Mifflin when the British opened an artillery barrage. Paine also joined scouting parties to ferret out key intelligence and was with Greene when he abandoned Fort Mercer, burning all the American ships to prevent their use by the advancing redcoats.

As winter began to take hold in December 1777, General Howe's forces settled snugly into the warm, comfortable confines of Philadelphia. Meanwhile, a grouchy Congress clamored from York, Pennsylvania, that General Washington move to retake and defend Philadelphia. But the commander in chief had to say no. By now, in the wake of defeats at Brandywine Creek and Germantown, the Continental Army was worn out, weary, and without supplies. It was imperative to rest and regroup. Washington then chose to locate his winter quarters at Valley Forge—a site only twenty miles northwest of Philadelphia—where he could again keep an eye on the British. Hard to take, but easily defended, Valley Forge was a heavily forested area, roughly two miles square, amid rolling hills along the edge of the Schuylkill River.

On December 19, 11,000 members of the American army literally staggered into the new encampment. Most of the men were between twenty and twenty-four years of age, with an average height of five feet, seven inches. They represented many of the states and dozens of vocations—from farmers to lawyers, from bakers to craftsmen. Upon their arrival, they were cold, hungry, destitute. Most had only one shirt, many had none. Thousands had no hats, no coats, no shoes, no socks. Hundreds more had to be carried or helped by their comrades because they were too sick to walk by themselves. Washington stated that "you might have tracked the army from White Marsh to Valley Forge by the blood of their feet."

There was no shelter at the campsite and nothing to eat. For the first few months, every meal consisted of "firecake"— a breadlike mixture of flour and water baked over an open campfire. At night, the men would sometimes cry out, "No meat. No meat." And, with a sense of humor, others would join in with cat calls, bird calls, owl hoots, and crowing. During the harshest months of the winter, sometimes they did not even have firecake to eat.

Out of necessity and in part to keep the soldiers occupied, Washington set them to building small huts. Each was to be the same size: fourteen by sixteen feet wide, six and one half feet high, "sides and ends made with logs," roofed with "split slabs." Washington also instructed that each hut be plastered with clay including an eighteen-inch clay fireplace. "I was there when the army first began to build huts," wrote Thomas Paine to Benjamin Franklin. "They appeared to me like a family of beavers, everyone busy, some carrying logs, others mud, and the rest plastering them together . . . a curious collection of buildings, in a true rustic order."

General Washington promised to share the soldier's hardships—eating firecake and sleeping in his tent until most of the huts were finished. Upon completion, twelve soldiers were assigned to every hut. There were no doors, no windows, and the smoke from the fireplace constantly burned the men's eyes. Then Washington instituted a systematic routine of discipline: ordering the men out of their huts at 5:00 each morning for exercise; sending them on minor missions to gather firewood; inspecting the troops frequently; and instituting courts-martial and flogging for those who disobeyed orders. And still Washington thought about constantly disrupting the enemy, but as he wrote just before Christmas 1777: "All I could do under these circumstances was to send out a few light parties to watch and harass the enemy."

When Washington heard that the Congress believed there were plenty of provisions in the neighborhood of Valley Forge, he immediately began a barrage of letters to enlighten them of his situation. He pleaded for food, told delegates that there was the very real danger of mutiny and desertion, and informed them that the delegates themselves were partly responsible for conditions existing at the camp. "I am now convinced beyond a doubt," Washington wrote, "that unless some great and capital change suddenly takes place, this army must inevitably be reduced to one or other of these three things. Starve, dissolve or disperse, in order to obtain subsistence in the best manner they can."

Congress, rather than helping, came to be something of a thorn in Washington's side. Some delegates continually attempted to smear and discredit him. In what was called the "Conway Cabal," General Thomas Conway even wrote a letter that impugned Washington's character and implied that General Horatio Gates should be placed in total command. As a result, Washington was forced to defend himself by writing a series of communiqués to Congress, to Conway, and to Gates. He chastised his two generals and invited members of Congress to visit Valley Forge and view the situation for themselves. But he could not and would not leave his men in such a dire situation.

Also, in mid-January, Congress ordered Washington to direct what they termed "an incursion into Canada." When the commander in chief refused, they ordered newly commissioned General Marie-Joseph du Motier (the Marquis de Lafayette) to proceed with the expedition to Canada along with General Conway. But Lafayette, who just the previous summer had arrived in Philadelphia to volunteer his services to the American cause, also refused to serve with Conway and threatened to return to France. In addition, he wrote Congress and advised them that their incursion into Canada idea was ridiculous. Lafayette and Washington had formed a close personal relationship—and they believed in each other completely.

Washington's concern for the men's welfare did not go unnoticed—and they became more dedicated and loyal to him as the winter wore on. He, in turn, was well aware that they were both despondent and devoted to the cause. "To see men without clothes to cover their nakedness," Washington wrote, "without blankets to lie on, without shoes . . . and submitting without a murmur, is a proof of patience and obedience which in my opinion can scarce be paralleled."

It soon became obvious to everyone at Valley Forge that, if they were to pull out of this desperate situation, they would have to do it without the help of their government. They knew they would have to pull together as a team and do it themselves.

Washington started the ball rolling by appointing General Nathanael Greene the new quartermaster general of the Continental Army. Greene, in turn, immediately sent out foraging parties to neighboring states and even into some of the southern states. Anthony Wayne went into New Jersey and scavenged along the river. Henry Lee rode all the way to Delaware and Maryland for food and supplies. And Alexander Hamilton raided British supplies near Philadelphia.

When local citizens realized the desperate situation at Valley Forge, they began to pitch in and lend a helping hand. Farmers brought in "meat, flour, potatoes, cabbage, and other foods, together with straw and clothing." A woman known only as Mrs. Bowers frequently rode into camp with her saddlebags full of food for the soldiers. Because he produced shoes for the troops, a cobbler named Bernard Fell was expelled from the Quaker meeting and suffered the humiliation and risk of having the British post a reward for his capture as a traitor. Martha Washington, George's wife, showed up at the encampment in February and immediately organized the wives of other officers to knit socks, patch pants, and make shirts. It was Nathanael Greene who constantly scrounged for cloth so that the women had material to work with.

And the soldiers themselves pulled together and helped each other. As more than 2,000 men were without shoes or boots, a shoemaker-turned-soldier not only kept busy making shoes, but taught others to do so as well. When a few sentries were seen standing barefoot in old hats, soldiers immediately set up a system where all lookouts were unselfishly lent whatever items of clothing they needed to keep warm.

After Washington had addressed the important issues of food and shelter for the army, he turned his attention to training—hoping to utilize the quiet winter months as an opportunity to mold the men into a better fighting machine. To accomplish the task, he appointed Inspector general a forty-seven-year-old Prussian named Frederick William Augustus Henry Ferdinand, Baron von Steuben.

Steuben, who had just arrived in America with a letter of recommendation from Benjamin Franklin, had served with Frederick the Great as a drill instructor and aide-de-camp. He arrived at Valley Forge in late February and placed himself at General Washington's disposal. The American commander then assigned Alexander Hamilton and John Laurens to act as aides to Steuben—and also ordered one hundred men to serve as a model company. The Prussian immediately set about creating a drill manual, but because he could not speak English, he wrote out the drills in French and then had a young Frenchman translate them into English. The instructions were subsequently reproduced so that there were enough copies to go around.

Steuben later recalled his first impressions of the army: "The men were literally naked," he observed, "some of them in the fullest extent of the word. The officers who had coats had them of every color and make. I saw officers mounting guard in a sort of dressing gown made of an old blanket or woolen bed cover."

As they set about training, Steuben and the soldiers developed a fondness and respect for each other—Steuben because he was impressed with the men's courage and fortitude; the troops because they were amused by the cantankerous old coot. When drilling the men, Steuben had to memorize his commands in English. But his heavy accent and faulty memory caused confusion and, when he became frustrated, he swore at the soldiers in three different languages. The veterans laughed out loud when he erupted in bursts of profanity—but they had respect for his efforts and did what he asked of them.

To a friend in Europe, Baron von Steuben wrote about his admiration for the American soldiers and the difference in their attitudes from European military men. "In the first place," he stated, "the genius of this nation is not in the least to be compared with that of the Prussians, Austrians, or French. You say to your soldier, 'Do this,' and he does it, but I am obliged to say, 'This is the reason why you ought to do that,' and he does it."

By late March, the once-emaciated soldiers were well clothed, well drilled, and noticeably putting on weight. One officer who kept a journal recorded that "the army grows stronger every day. It increases in numbers and there is a spirit of discipline among the troops that is better than numbers. Each brigade is on parade almost every day for several hours [marching] with regularity and exactness."

On March 21, Thomas Paine published the fifth installment of *The American Crisis*. It was, as he said later, designed to improve Washington's reputation and inspire the enlistment of new volunteers. In the essay, Paine audaciously proposed drafting four out of every one hundred men for military service—with the other ninety-six contributing money and services to the cause. Shortly thereafter, Congress put out a call for volunteers and authorized General Washington to call up 5,000 members of the militias from Maryland, New Jersey, and Pennsylvania. By late May, new recruits were flooding into Valley Forge to become trained members of the now-renewed Continental Army. And by mid-June, Washington had 13,500 men at his disposal.

During the six months at Valley Forge, 3,000 men died of starvation and disease—nearly one in four. Many lost limbs from severe frostbite, and all witnessed their comrades suffer unimaginable hardships. And yet those who survived that fateful winter later pointed to Valley Forge as the turning point of the American Revolution.

Through teamwork, optimism, and courage, the veterans had pulled together and transformed themselves from a rag-tag lot into a fine fighting force. And, in the process, they became a tight-knit team of inspired patriots committed to a glorious cause. John Marshall of Virginia, later Chief Justice of the United States, was to write: "I found myself associated with brave men from different states who were risking their life and everything valuable in a common cause. I was confirmed in the habit of considering America as my country."

George Washington had pulled off an amazing turnaround by combining an optimistic attitude with a grounded reality in what the situation was—and what had to be done to rectify it. He was on the spot the entire time, fighting for his people, encouraging them, living as they lived, walking among them. He listened and acted decisively when it counted. And, more importantly, George Washington never gave up hope.

THE FOUNDING FATHERS ON LEADERSHIP

★ When the competition thinks you're down for the count, you have an opportunity to achieve a major victory.
★ March while the competition is sleeping.
★ Ride to the front and motion for the troops to follow.
★ Rest when necessary, but stay close to the competition so as to keep a watchful eye on their actions.
★ There is a three-to-one advantage in favor of the proactive party.
★ Constantly communicate your situation to those who may render support.
★ Stick around when others flee. Stay near the action.
★ Keep your sense of humor, even during the worst moments of crisis.
★ Share the hardships of the people you lead.
★ Fight for your honor when it is attacked.
★ Pull together as a team and take responsibility for your own situation.
★ Combine an optimistic attitude with a grounded reality in what the situation is—and what must be done to rectify it.
★ Never give up hope.

> "Were I to fight a battle, I should be cut to pieces, the militia dispersed and the arms lost. Were I to decline fighting, the country would think itself given up. I am therefore determined to skirmish, but not to engage too far. . . . When the fate of America may be at stake on the issue, I cannot think it safe or wise to adopt a different system. . . . If, under the circumstances, I am able to keep above water, I'll be happy."
>
> George Washington, 1778

8 / Harass, Innovate, and Leverage Resources

TEAM LEADERS
George Washington
George Rogers Clark
"Light Horse" Harry Lee
Francis "Swamp Fox" Marion
General Daniel Morgan
Thomas "Gamecock" Sumter
"Mad" Anthony Wayne

George Washington was astonishingly successful in managing the meager resources of thirteen small colonies against those of the great British empire. From the very beginning, he was at a disadvantage in nearly every aspect of warfare. Colonial weaponry was far less sophisticated, for instance. Americans lacked the manufacturing capability of the British—and had to rely almost solely on captured enemy supplies. They did not have endless reserves of soldiers—nor the funding to engage mercenary-for-hire foreigners as King George had done with the Hessians. And with young, inexperienced troops who might not be depended upon to hold their positions in an open confrontation, the Americans were reluctant to place troops "on open ground against those who were superior both in number and in discipline."

Accordingly, Washington's strategy was to concentrate his strength and not engage the enemy directly if he could help it. "On our side the war should be defensive," he wrote Congress in 1776. "It has even been called a 'war of posts.' That we should on all occasions avoid a general action, [and not] put anything to the risk, unless compelled by a necessity." Clearly, the general was concerned as much about keeping his army intact as he was about winning military victories—perhaps more so. "Were I to fight a battle," he privately told Lafayette in 1778, "I should be cut to pieces, the militia dispersed and the arms lost. Were I to decline fighting, the country would think itself given up. I am therefore determined to skirmish, but not to engage too far."

But George Washington was also well aware of the great risk such a strategy might cause to the morale of the public at large—not to mention his own reputation. "I know the unhappy predicament I stand in. . . ." he said. "I am sensible enough to know that a retreating army is encircled with difficulties, that declining an engagement subjects a general to reproach and that the common cause may be in some measure affected by the discouragements which it throws over the minds of many. [However], when the fate of America may be at stake on the issue, I cannot think it safe or wise to adopt a different system. . . . If, under the circumstances, I am able to keep above water, I'll be happy."

During the first three years of the war, George Washington lost five of seven major battles. The rest of the fighting in which he engaged the Continental Army was in the form of minor skirmishes and harassing raids. All through the Revolution, Washington sent out foraging parties to chafe the

British. He ordered intermittent raids designed to keep the enemy on edge and disrupt their operations. Often, they'd hit by surprise in the middle of the night, or take potshots during the day from behind trees. And before the redcoats could assemble and strike back, the Americans took to their heels and were gone.

Because he could not beat the greatest military power on earth, George Washington's strategy was to wear them down, wait them out, and frustrate the heck out of their leadership. And by 1779, there were clear signs that his strategy was working. For example, American patriots were constantly raiding Long Island from their base in Norwalk, Connecticut—usually ambushing British supply boats. It was this harassment that unnerved and angered General Clinton so greatly that he had Norwalk burned to the ground. When word got around of what had happened, it made Americans all the more angry and committed to the cause.

Washington's tactics also included making it appear that the American army was larger than it actually was. Hundreds and hundreds of small groups harassing the enemy made it seem as though his troops were literally everywhere—all the time. And when General Washington marched his army through the streets of Philadelphia during the summer of 1777, he strung out the parade as long and as far as he possibly could in order to make the local Tory sympathizers believe that he, indeed, possessed an overwhelming force. Washington ordered the men to march in a single column slowly through town. And, as John Adams recorded in his diary: "They took twelve hours in passing by. They were extremely well armed, pretty well clothed, and tolerably disciplined. Their drums were beating and their fifers were shrilling 'Yankee Doodle.' "

A gathering of the Continental Army's top executive military advisers took place at Valley Forge on June 17, 1778. Present were George Washington and sixteen others, including Greene, Wayne, Hamilton, Lafayette, General Charles

Lee, and Baron von Steuben. The leaders discussed what appeared to be, from all intelligence reports, the enemy's intention to evacuate Philadelphia. If the British did not plan to "march through Jersey," said Washington, "they have been making a deal of useless preparation . . . [by] the great number of horses and carriages they have been collecting with so much industry."

While Nathanael Greene and Anthony Wayne urged an all-out attack, others, led by General Lee, preferred a more cautious wait-and-see approach. Steuben, however, advised Washington to nip at the enemy while they were on the move and strung out. Lafayette concurred and further pointed out that with more than 10,000 troops and 1,500 wagons, the redcoat column would stretch for miles along the New Jersey landscape.

As the council was divided, General Washington broke the logjam when he decided to pursue the British and wait for favorable opportunities to strike—all the while trying to avoid a large-scale battle. "Frequently," Washington said, "the most effectual way to defend is to attack." Essentially, though, he agreed with Lafayette and Steuben that the thing to do was to stick with his basic strategy and harass the British.

The next morning, on June 18, the king's troops, led now by Sir Henry Clinton (who had replaced Howe), left Philadelphia for New York City without fanfare. As one resident put it: "They did not go away, they vanished." In a matter of days, the entire Continental Army—with a new strength and a new attitude—left Valley Forge and crossed the Delaware River in hot pursuit.

The British trek quickly became a miles-long narrow column—often with significant gaps in the chain. Washington dispatched small groups to cut down bridges and snipe at the enemy all along their line while his main army followed close enough to be ready for a major skirmish—but not so close as to be surprised and outflanked. The weather was hot and muggy—a typical New Jersey summer. Each British soldier carried a sixty-pound backpack and marched in heavy red woolen uniforms. Many suffered heat stroke and several died during the trek. It didn't take long before the American harassment teams were picking up stragglers and deserters.

Late on the afternoon of June 26, the front of the British column reached Monmouth Court House in northern New Jersey; the rest of the troops meandered in throughout the evening. To a man, they were almost totally exhausted, a fact of which General Washington was well aware, not only through key intelligence reports but also because some of his own men had been collapsing from the heat. If ever there was going to be an opportunity to strike a major blow, thought Washington, surely this was it.

At four o'clock on the morning of June 28, patriot spotters reported that Clinton's advance column was beginning to march out of Monmouth Court House. At dawn, Washington gave the order for General Charles Lee's forward division to attack the British rear guard (commanded by Cornwallis). But the attack quickly turned into mass confusion when it became apparent that Lee had not coordinated the action with his troops. As Cornwallis wheeled his men around, the Americans began a retreat while Lee apparently told another officer that he had "orders from Congress and the commander-in-chief not to engage."

Meanwhile, a colonel in the militia rode back to the main force to inform Washington that the army was in full retreat. "By whose orders are the troops retreating?" asked the general.

"By General Lee's," came the reply.

"Damn him!" said Washington as he spurred his horse and galloped off.

In a short time the two leaders met—Washington riding toward the sound of the guns, Lee riding in the opposite direction. "My God, General Lee!" thundered Washington. "What is the reason for this disorder and confusion?"

When Lee began to rattle off a series of excuses, General

Washington is said to have shouted and sworn " 'till the leaves shook on the trees." "Whatever your opinions might have been," he said to Lee, "I expected my orders would have been obeyed."

Washington then took control. He rode up and down the ranks, first turning the troops around and then lining them up. Anthony Wayne positioned his men behind hedges at the front and others formed on his flanks in solid defensive positions. The British, led by a cavalry charge from Cornwallis and joined by Clinton's main army, attacked in force—but the American volleys pushed them back. The battle lasted all day. Finally, when it became dark, the redcoats retreated to defensive positions.

That night, the Continental Army slept in place with their guns by their sides and General Washington passed the word that his intention was to attack at first light. The next morning, however, the entire British army was gone. Taking a tactic from Washington's own playbook, General Clinton realized his men were too weary to win a major battle and quietly pulled out in the middle of the night. Within two days, the British were safely ensconced in New York City. General Washington, in turn, followed along and eventually took up positions in a ring around the city hoping to hem in and, at the same time, keep an eye on the main British force.

The battle of Monmouth Court House turned out to be the last major battle of the American Revolution to take place in the northern colonies. It was essentially a draw, with both sides suffering about 400 casualties. After the fight, General Washington gave Anthony Wayne a commendation and arrested General Lee, who was found guilty in a general court-martial and suspended from the army for one year.

Of George Washington's actions at Monmouth Court House, the Marquis de Lafayette marveled: "His presence stopped the retreat," he wrote. "His fine appearance on horseback, his calm courage, roused to animation . . . gave him the air best calculated to excite enthusiasm. He rode all along the lines amid the shouts of the soldiers, cheering them by his voice and example and restoring to our standard the fortunes of the fight."

For the second half of 1778, both sides avoided making any major attacks against the other. The British felt safe and well protected in New York. It was almost as if they did not know how to react or what to do when confronted with such unorthodox harassment tactics—so they remained inactive. And the Americans, unable to take the city, were content to wait patiently.

George Washington's leadership style to this point in the American Revolution may be something of a guide to all small organizations who are attempting to compete against giants. He constantly kept changing his position so as not to be outflanked. And he knew all the time exactly what the competition was up to so that he could react quickly and effectively. His ongoing program of harassment, of making small dents as opposed to attempting major wreckage, also had the effect of trying the patience of the competition. In business, it might be equated to a smaller, more agile company stealing customers from a major corporation heavily laden with bureaucracy. In local government, it might be a small town fighting a neighboring larger city's airport expansion. And in sports, it might be a young, peppery baseball team squeezing runs in one by one against a team heavily laden with power hitters and high-priced superstars.

If an organization looks at its situation as a long-term project, as a nine-inning game, then an effective strategy can be to chip away at the competition, picking up markets, points, and allies along the way. Such a long-term viewpoint serves to foster patience and perseverance. If things don't go well in the first few innings, you still have seven or eight more chances to catch up and turn it around.

Another tactic George Washington and the American colonies pursued effectively was to leverage the meager assets they had at their disposal. They made due with what they had, stretched everything to the limit, and scrounged for more. By extending the use of supplies, they saved massive expenditures for new material. And by scrounging up what was already available, and then converting it to something usable, they not only saved money, but the time it would take to build, acquire, or transport weapons and other military necessities.

The tents George Washington pitched at Dorchester Heights in 1775 were the same tents he pitched at Yorktown in 1781. And when the Continental Army first left home with only the clothes on their backs, by the time they reached Valley Forge, their clothes had literally rotted off their bodies. As a matter of fact, uniforms were virtually nonexistent for most of the war, so Washington ordered his regular soldiers to wear a piece of evergreen in their hats for distinction. He had major generals wear purple ribbons on their chests, brigadiers pink, and aides-de-camp green. Captains, in turn, wore yellow in their hats, sergeants wore red on their shoulders, and corporals wore green.

One of the most impressive examples of how Washington and the Americans leveraged resources involved their tactics in combating Great Britain's overwhelming sea power. The Royal Navy controlled not only the seas, but most of the rivers, lakes, and coastal communities as well. It was an unusually powerful advantage because all but one of the original thirteen colonies were easily accessed from the Atlantic Ocean.

At the beginning of the war, America had no official navy. There were, however, a great many ships employed in the private sector by businesses involved in both domestic and foreign trade—and there were thousands of people manning those ships. George Washington actively encouraged privateers to join the cause and, in addition, pressed the Continental Congress to help them get organized.

Delegates did form a committee headed by John Adams for the express purpose of "fitting out armed vessels," which eventually led to the formation of the first American navy. With time, the Continental Congress also set up regional naval Boards of Admiralty. In general, though, the loose collection of vessels was affectionately termed "Washington's Navy." Its main contributions during the war involved transporting supplies, keeping America's trade going while disrupting that of Great Britain, and, once in a while, seizing British ships and the cargo on board.

During the early years of conflict, the American colonies were able to come up with thirteen frigates—none of which lasted through the Revolution. By contrast, the British increased their number of ships from 270 at the beginning of the war to 468 at the end. However, innovative tactics by people manning American vessels did have a positive cumulative effect. For instance, on July 15, 1779, when three American ships became lost in a dense fog in waters off Newfoundland, they found themselves (after the weather cleared) in the middle of 150 British merchant ships protected by only one warship. The American captains passed themselves off as British ships and ended up capturing eleven of the merchant vessels and more than a million dollars' worth of cargo.

George Washington's innovative and unconventional tactics throughout the war served to set the tone and inspire other, like-minded creative officers and soldiers to do the same. When they saw their leader maneuver at night and launch surprise attacks, they tried it. When they saw him break tradition and wage campaigns in the winter, they followed his lead. And when they finally understood his harassment strategy—and the subsequent British labeling of it as "assassination tactics"—local military leaders throughout all the colonies began imitating Washington's creative style.

Down in South Carolina, Colonel Francis Marion, better known as "The Swamp Fox," and General Thomas Sumter, nicknamed "The Gamecock," constantly nipped at the heels of the British infantry. Marion operated from remote swamps staying on the move so the British could not catch him. He employed hit-and-run tactics and never commanded more than a few hundred men at any one time. Sumter employed similar innovative tactics that often resulted in the capture of supplies, horses, and prisoners. Together, they also significantly disrupted British communications, in part by intercepting dispatch riders.

At Haw River, North Carolina, twenty-year-old Colonel Henry "Light Horse Harry" Lee (father of the Civil War's Robert E. Lee) and his select mounted infantry daringly approached 400 British loyalists on horseback. Lee audaciously passed himself off as British General Banastre Tarleton (both Tarleton's men and Lee's men wore green dragoon coats). When the loyalists put down their weapons and stepped aside, Lee's Legion rode in among them with sabers drawn and then killed or captured the entire division.

Out in Illinois, George Rogers Clark marched 200 men through swamps and dense forests and waded through shoulder-deep lake waters to sneak up on British-occupied Vincennes. After arriving on the outskirts of town, he sent in a captured prisoner with word that he planned to attack the fort that evening. His message also warned British sympathizers to leave town and residents who favored the American cause to remain indoors. Clark then split his small force into two divisions to give the appearance that he had a larger force and started his move toward Vincennes. The ploy worked, as most of the locals either fled or brought him extra supplies. And by attacking at night, the redcoats inside the fort did not sense that the force attacking them was small and scattered. When the British surrendered the fort the next morning, Clark had succeeded in the first of his campaign to wrest the northwestern territories from British control and place them under the American flag. He later concluded similar campaigns in Kentucky and Ohio, and even helped keep Spanish-controlled St. Louis from being overtaken by the British.

Throughout the Revolution, Americans improvised and innovated. And several leading generals thought of new ways to motivate their troops. At the battle of Stony Point, New York, for instance, "Mad" Anthony Wayne began to earn his nickname when he actually offered $500 cash prizes to the first five men who entered the British-occupied fort. Wayne then sent groups of men with axes up to the walls of the garrison to chop through the wooden columns. Following them were squads of twenty soldiers surging through the holes to engage the redcoats in hand-to-hand combat. After the British surrendered, Wayne sent General Washington this message: "The fort and garrison are ours. Our officers and men behaved like men who are determined to be free."

At the battle of the Cowpens, South Carolina, in 1781, General Daniel Morgan came up with a brilliant military tactic designed to neutralize the tendency of American militiamen to break and run when under heavy pressure. He placed his militia troops in two front lines and ordered them to fire no more than two volleys—and then run to the rear behind the Continental regulars. The night before the battle, Morgan walked from campfire to campfire to reassure and remind his men of their assignments. "Remember, boys," he told them, "just hold up your heads, give them two fires and you're free." During the battle, the militia did as they were told and the redcoats, believing they were winning, charged wildly right into the path of the entrenched Americans. Nearly 80 percent of the British force was killed or captured that day— marking one of the great military successes in the south.

Southerners, in particular, really took to George Washington's innovative tactics. As a matter of fact, they started banding together in an effort to leverage their resources and come up with even more creative ways to beat the British. For example, Light Horse Harry Lee's cavalry brigade joined up with the Swamp Fox and Marion's Brigade to take several key redcoat outposts. At Fort Motte, they forced a quick surrender by firing flaming arrows inside the walls. And when stalled at a siege of Fort Watson, one of their men, Colonel Hezekiah Maham, invented a unique contraption, later called the

"Maham Tower," that forced a surrender in a matter of days. The innovative colonel built a tall rectangular box with a platform on top—and then placed militia marksmen on it so that they could fire over the walls of the fort. The same technique was used the next month to take the British outpost at Augusta, Georgia.

George Washington not only allowed such innovative tactics—he actively *encouraged* them. His strategy was to inspire Americans everywhere to act on their own—to do what they could to disrupt, to delay, and to defeat the British. He was smart enough to realize he could not do it all himself. So, faced with a formidable adversary, one that nearly everyone felt was unbeatable, George Washington chose to make the war unwinnable for them, and then to wait for them to realize it. Washington's style, in turn, led to innovation, creativity, and the maximum leveraging of resources. That's how a small organization can compete against a larger one—with patience, perseverance, innovation.

Essentially, George Washington told his people: "We can't beat them in the short term. So let's be in it for the long term. Let's harass 'em to death."

THE FOUNDING FATHERS ON LEADERSHIP

★ When outnumbered, put nothing at risk unless compelled by necessity.

★ When confronted with an overwhelming power, wear them down, wait them out, and frustrate the heck out of their leadership.

★ Employ tactics that make your organization seem larger than it is.

★ When your advisers are divided, break the logjam with a decision and move forward.

★ Frequently, the most effective way to defend is to attack.

★ When the competition is exhausted and weak—strike!

★ After a major engagement, reward those who acted well and "court-martial" those who acted unacceptably.

★ Chip away at the competition—picking up markets, points, and allies along the way.

★ Leverage the assets at your disposal. Make do with what you have, stretch everything to the limit, and scrounge for more.

★ When you employ innovative and unconventional tactics, you inspire like-minded people to do the same.

★ Don't simply allow creativity and innovation; *encourage* it.

★ Be smart enough to realize that you can't do it all yourself.

PART III

WINNING THE WAR

"We have not yet applied to any foreign power for assistance, nor offered our commerce for their friendship. . . . Yet it is natural to think of it, if we are pressed."

Benjamin Franklin, 1775

"Assure Congress of my friendship. I hope this will be for the good of the two nations."

King Louis XVI to Benjamin Franklin after formally recognizing the Treaty of Alliance between France and the United States, March 20, 1778

"Your Majesty may count on the gratitude of Congress and its faithful observance of the pledges it now takes."

Benjamin Franklin's reply to the king, March 20, 1778

9 / Build Strong Alliances

TEAM LEADER
Benjamin Franklin

In the spring of 1777, the first of many shipments of aid from France arrived in America. This consignment included 8,750 pairs of shoes, 48,000 pairs of socks, 3,600 blankets, and 4,000 tents. In addition to much-needed personal necessities, there was a tremendous supply of weapons, including: 37,000 rifles, 373,000 flints, half a million musket balls, hundreds of mortars and grenades, and 161,000 pounds of gun-powder.

While France valued their economic trade relationship with the colonies, there was another, more overriding reason to provide support—they wanted to take the British down a notch or two. The French had suffered a crushing defeat at the hands of the British in 1763—ending the Seven Years' War (of which the French and Indian War was a minor part). So they were, in no small degree, motivated by revenge. But the newly appointed French foreign minister, the Comte de Vergennes (who came to power in 1774 when Louis XVI ascended the throne), also astutely realized that should Americans succeed in their revolution, Great Britain's world economic leadership would wane significantly. After all, much of their wealth and power emanated from the colonies. Conversely, the British leadership greatly feared an entrance of France into the war. Not only would it be costly (the Seven Years' War left England with a serious national debt), but hostilities with the French would result in having to fight on more than one front, including the West Indies and a variety of other places around the world.

Of course, this was a fact of which the founding fathers were well aware. Early in the conflict, Benjamin Franklin was thinking strategically about such an alliance when, in 1775, he wrote to a friend: "We have not yet applied to any foreign power for assistance, nor offered our commerce for their friendship. . . . Yet it is natural to think of it, if we are pressed." The British occupation of Boston and the battles of Bunker Hill and Breed's Hill provided all the "pressing" that Franklin would need. At his urging, Congress set up their five-man secret Committee of Correspondence, which was specifically charged with "corresponding with our friends in other parts of the world." Franklin chaired the committee and served with Jefferson, John Dickinson, John Jay, Benjamin Harrison, and Robert Morris.

During their first year in existence, the group concentrated mostly on securing funding and arms for the American forces. In July 1776, for instance, they commissioned Connecticut businessman Silas Deane to travel to Paris and purchase military supplies from the French. It was Deane who was chiefly responsible for securing the first consignment of supplies to arrive the next spring. In addition, Franklin immediately sent out letters to various governments testing the waters as to whether they might be inclined to enter into a permanent alliance. They frequently appealed to Canada, for example, to join the American union. A formal direct appeal was made in mid-1775, and when the Articles of Confederation were drafted in 1776, Congress included a provision admitting Canada to the union should they desire to join.

In general, though, America's leaders knew that their strategy of building foreign alliances would have to be a long-term effort of effective public relations and diplomacy. They further realized that the key to getting things going was to get France into the war. And the key to persuading France to join the effort rested largely in the hands of one man—Benjamin Franklin. Congress felt that people needed to be in France, on the ground, building relationships and working the decision-makers. So, they appointed Franklin, Deane, and Thomas Jefferson to lead the effort. When Jefferson refused, he was accused by some of his colleagues of preferring the easy life to serving his country. In fact, Jefferson's wife, Martha, was pregnant and he had resigned his seat in Congress to be with her.

On December 21, 1776, Franklin arrived in Paris (joining American commissioners Silas Deane and Arthur Lee, Jefferson's replacement) with direction from his government to negotiate treaties, seek loans, and procure ships for the American cause. Congress also wanted him to "press for the immediate and explicit declaration of France in our favor." But the wise old Philadelphian knew it was not going to be that easy. It would involve a lot of patience, time, and relationship-building. And for the next nine years, he stayed in Europe to achieve this most crucial of missions for his country.

In France, Franklin was nothing less than charismatic. He was a great conversationalist who spoke in natural, straightforward language—yet with elegance and grace. In essence, he charmed the French with his personal demeanor. And they were also fascinated by his combination of supreme intellectual capacity and backwoods simplicity. Actually, by the time Benjamin Franklin arrived in Paris, he was already a worldrenowned scientist, journalist, and philosopher. As John Adams wrote: "There was scarcely a peasant or a citizen, a valet de chambre, coachman or footman, a lady's chambermaid or a scullion in a kitchen, who was not familiar with [Franklin], and who did not consider him as a friend to human kind."

Benjamin Franklin stepped forward to help lead the American Revolution because of his inbred sense of right versus wrong, because he was passionate, and because he knew he could make a difference. Diplomacy was clearly Franklin's forte. He was the perfect individual to assume the lead in international alliance-building—and all the other founding fathers knew it. They bowed to his advice and opinions when push came to shove and they followed his lead. He was, after all, the most accomplished of all the men who had signed the Declaration of Independence. He was a scientist who had made important discoveries in electricity. He was an inventor—of the rocking chair, bifocal glasses, and the Franklin stove. He had organized the first volunteer fire department, the first city police force, and the first postal system in America. And Ben Franklin was a scholar of the most eminent degree. He had taught himself five languages, was known as the "Isaac Newton of his Age," wrote the world-famous *Poor Richard's Almanac* from 1732 to 1757, and had founded the University of Pennsylvania. But this man was no Poor Richard himself. Before leaving for Paris, he loaned the nearly bankrupt American government £4,000 out of his own pocket.

Franklin, who had also served a stint as the president of Pennsylvania, was born the fifteenth of seventeen children to a candlestick maker and his wife. He began his apprenticeship as a printer at the age of twelve and, when he was about that age, he drew up a list of thirteen virtues which he attempted to achieve. The list included such things as: "lose no time"; "wrong no one"; "avoid extremes"; and "cultivate humility." Franklin kept this list of virtues with him everywhere he went for the rest of his life.

For all his skill and ability, though, the success of Franklin's assignment in France would depend in large part on George Washington's success on the battlefield. The French government was reluctant to do much of anything at first except ship arms and supplies—and then only in secret and through middlemen. They also informed America's new ambassador that they would not enter into an alliance with America unless Spain also agreed to enter.

France's reasoning for caution and timidity in the early going was understandable. They had just lost a war to England and did not want to lose another. It was preferable for them to wait until it looked as though the Americans actually had the potential to win their revolution. But, in 1775, 1776, and the first three quarters of 1777, the situation looked bleak indeed. Hearing that Washington had lost New York, been pushed back through New Jersey, and then had lost Philadelphia was difficult for Franklin to relay to the French. He knew that small, hit-and-run victories like Trenton and Princeton would not persuade the French to enter the war. They were waiting for a major victory.

But Franklin remained optimistic, even when he received a letter from his daughter advising him that she had fled Philadelphia. "Your library we sent out of town," she wrote, "well packed in boxes, a week before us; and all the valuable things, we brought with us." When he was finally told that

General Howe had captured Philadelphia, Franklin instantly snapped: "No, Philadelphia has captured Howe!"

At virtually the same moment he heard of the British occupation of his hometown, Franklin also was informed of America's great military victory at Saratoga, New York. General Horatio Gates, prodded by Generals Benedict Arnold and Daniel Morgan, had pursued British commander Johnny Burgoyne's troops to the heights of Saratoga. The redcoats had been on the road for months, their numbers had dwindled seriously, and they were desperately short of food and supplies. On the other hand, Gates's army was numerous and well fed—having received almost the entire initial French consignment of supplies. The Americans outnumbered the British at Saratoga by more than two to one (13,000 to 6,000). Realizing there was no hope of either victory or reinforcement, Burgoyne, on October 17, 1777, laid down his arms and surrendered his entire army. And General Gates, in an almost unheard-of concession, granted free passage to England for all of the defeated British troops.

The Continental Congress quickly sent an envoy to Paris to inform Benjamin Franklin and the French of the important victory. Upon hearing the dramatic news, Franklin realized it was what he had been waiting for and pounced on the opportunity. He immediately drafted a note to Foreign Minister Vergennes: "We have the honor to acquaint your Excellency that we have just received an express from Boston with advice of the total reduction of the force under General Burgoyne, himself, and his whole army having surrendered themselves prisoners."

When word spread around Paris of the American victory, open celebrations took place in the streets and Franklin and other Americans were heartily congratulated wherever they went. The next day, when Vergennes sent his personal congratulations and invited a renewal of the American request for a formal alliance with France, Franklin quickly sat down and drafted a proposal. "The commissioners from the Congress of the United States of North America," he began, "beg leave to represent to your excellency, that it is near a year since they had the honor of putting into your hands the propositions of Congress for a treaty of amity and commerce with this kingdom." The document went on to request military aid from France in return for a guarantee that America would "make no peace [with] Great Britain" but, rather, "should declare war against them."

Meanwhile, news of Burgoyne's defeat at Saratoga had caused panic and hysteria in the streets and government houses of London. Lord North, Britain's prime minister, sent an emissary to Paris and requested a meeting with Benjamin Franklin to pursue an end to hostilities. The American would be offered a safe-conduct pass to London to discuss what terms the United States would accept, short of independence. Further, Lord North offered a repeal of all laws to which the colonies had objected.

But as he wanted to see exactly what the French were going to do, Franklin kept North's emissary cooling his heels in a waiting room for nearly two weeks. The answer came in mid-December when the Comte de Vergennes sent a secret coach to transport Franklin and the other American emissaries to Versailles for a conference. Once there, they were informed that France would, indeed, recognize the United States and enter into a broad-based military and economic alliance on the condition that Spain be asked to join. Later, when the Spanish government declined, Vergennes opted to move forward without them. At that point, Franklin called in Lord North's emissary, categorically refused to travel to London for peace talks, and sent him back to London with the message that his country would never accept any peace plan that did not center around total independence.

Echoing that sentiment, the French Royal Council unanimously voted to approve treaties of amity and commerce with the United States. The Treaty of Alliance, which was signed on February 6, 1778, specifically called for the "absolute and unlimited independence of the United States." At the formal signing ceremony, Benjamin Franklin, who had almost single-handedly pulled off this diplomatic coup, wore the very same brown velvet suit he had worn in London in 1774 the day he was lectured in public by British Attorney General Alexander Wedderburn (in retaliation for the Boston Tea Party). A short time later France declared war on Great Britain—and Franklin never wore the suit again.

King Louis XVI then invited Franklin, Deane, and Lee to the palace at Versailles to formally recognize the treaties. "Assure Congress of my friendship," the king told Franklin. "I hope this will be for the good of the two nations."

"Your Majesty may count on the gratitude of Congress," replied Franklin, "and its faithful observance of the pledges it now takes."

Upon hearing of the treaty between America and France, Lord North appointed Frederick, Earl of Carlisle, to head to New York with a proposal of peace made directly to members of the Continental Congress. However, Congress not only refused to meet, it passed a resolution stating that any individual or group that might negotiate with the Carlisle Commission was an enemy of the United States.

Interestingly enough, Carlisle was authorized to offer not only a return to circumstances prior to the Sugar Act, but also American representation in Parliament and official recognition of the American Congress as a permanent entity. But it was too little, too late. When they were rebuked, members of the Carlisle Commission tried to bribe George Washington (through an intermediary) by offering him a dukedom. And British officials in France similarly tried to approach Franklin. These overtures were rejected immediately and Great Britain was left with absolutely no doubt as to the determination of the American patriots.

Back on the European scene, Benjamin Franklin was appointed to the high status of minister plenipotentiary to France, where his duties were largely to help coordinate military efforts between the French and American armies. In addition, other American diplomats arrived in Europe with assignments to build more foreign alliances. John Jay went to Spain; Arthur Lee to Prussia; his brother, William, to Austria; Francis Dana went to Russia; and John Adams arrived in Paris as Silas Deane's replacement to begin several years of service. Adams traveled widely, especially taking numerous trips to Amsterdam where he secured a $10 million loan and a treaty of commerce and friendship with the Dutch. With time, Spain also joined the cause.

In general, Benjamin Franklin's strategic alliance with France dramatically changed the direction and momentum of the American Revolution. Moreover, it resulted in four primary, and immediate, benefits to the American cause:

1. It strengthened forces and shored up a major weakness.

Thousands of professional French troops from the West Indies and France arrived in America to aid the Continental Army. They were far and away the best-dressed and best-equipped soldiers in the war, even outshining the British regulars. In addition, France brought a formidable naval force to the table, where America had only the far inferior, makeshift Washington's Navy.

2. It lifted morale and built courage.

Not only did the French alliance give Franklin and the Continental Congress confidence enough to slap British peace offerings in the face, it provided a major lift to the morale of American soldiers. When George Washington received the news at Valley Forge, he immediately passed word to the troops who were in training under Baron von Steuben—and then stated euphorically that the alliance meant the "certain prospect of success" for the American cause.

Also, members of the Continental Congress finally passed the Articles of Confederation and sent the document on to the states for "consideration and approbation." While the Articles were not perfect, they did provide the first vehicle dedicated to the concept of "perpetual union"—including provisions for the common defense, a common treasury and minting of coins and currency, election of congressional delegates, congressional approval of treaties, open borders, and freedom of speech. When delegates to the state legislatures received word of the French alliance, they gained more courage to ratify the Articles.

3. It added new markets.

French ports were now open and receptive to American ships all over the world, which, in turn, increased economic advantages. And once France declared war on Great Britain, other nations began to choose up sides—and those with French sympathies readily accepted American merchants. Essentially, the United States dramatically increased markets for its goods and services.

4. It diluted the competition.

When France entered into an alliance with the United States, Great Britain found itself involved in a world war rather than only an internal family squabble. As such, they could not afford to concentrate military efforts only in the colonies. Parliament ordered General Clinton to send 5,000 men to the West Indies and another 3,000 to St. Augustine and Pensacola in an effort to protect Florida. General Clinton was also forced to concentrate his main force in New York City where the Royal Navy could provide supply and defense. Clearly, the French alliance was the main reason for the British evacuation of Philadelphia. So when Benjamin Franklin achieved his goal in Paris, he also freed his hometown.

The French alliance with the United States not only served as formal recognition of America's independence, it also bitterly divided the people of Great Britain. A major faction, primarily comprised of the upper class with antiwar sentiments, suddenly became more vocal. These people were upset that they were not only losing revenue from American markets, but that they were now losing additional global markets because of a world war. And William Pitt, a leading dissident in Parliament, scolded his colleagues: "My lords, you cannot conquer America," he said. "[If I were they], I would never lay down my arms! Never! Never! Never!"

In their book *Leaders,* Warren Bennis and Bert Nanus noted that "leadership establishes trust" and that "leaders pay attention." Leaders also look ahead, plan for the future, and achieve goals for their organizations. Benjamin Franklin, by paying attention to the French and establishing trust with them, was able to forge one of the strongest political alliances in world history. In so doing, he added strength, resources, and a greater ability to leverage resources to the American cause. It took him years to get the job done. But by looking ahead and planning for the future, he was able to achieve one of the chief goals the founding fathers had set for themselves at the beginning of the conflict.

Not coincidentally, Franklin's efforts in the late eighteenth century were similar to strategies employed by business executives in the late twentieth century. As major corporations struggle to "go global," they have tended to "partner up," create joint ventures, and forge new strategic business relationships. By doing so, they are able to add strength to their own organizations, lift internal morale, access new global markets, and effectively dilute and outdistance their competition. In essence, building strong alliances—whether with individuals or groups—allows leaders to achieve more results for themselves and for their organizations.

THE FOUNDING FATHERS ON LEADERSHIP

★ It is natural to think of forming alliances, especially if you are pressed.

★ Set up a committee especially designed to pursue strategic alliances.

★ Send out letters to various organizations testing the waters as to whether they might be inclined to enter a joint venture.

★ Building alliances with other organizations must be a long-term effort involving effective public relations and diplomacy.

★ Try to remain optimistic even when things look bleakest.

★ Keep your eyes and ears open and pounce on your opportunity when it presents itself.

★ A key strategic alliance or joint venture has the potential to change the direction and the momentum of your revolution.

★ Pay attention and establish trust.

★ By looking ahead and planning for the future, you will be able to achieve your chief goals.

★ Building strategic alliances strengthens your forces, lifts morale, adds new markets, and dilutes the competition.

> "Every lover of his country must strain his credit. No time, my dear sir, is to be lost."
>
> > George Washington to Robert Morris, December 1776

> "I have now waded through a tedious course of difficult business, and over an untrodden path. The subject on every point . . . was entangled with perplexities and enveloped in obscurity, yet such are the resources of America, that she wants nothing but system to insure success."
>
> > Thomas Paine,
> > *The Crisis Extraordinary,*
> > October 4, 1780

10 / *Attend to Financial Matters*

TEAM LEADERS
Robert Morris
Thomas Paine

Even with windfall economic aid from France, financial problems plagued America throughout the entire Revolutionary War. Out-of-control inflation, a dramatic rise in the cost of living, the very real threat of bankruptcy, and a whopping national debt all constantly threatened to end the founding fathers' quest for independence.

And the problems were not easily solved. Indeed, many historians would claim that the situation never really was worked out until many years after the war had ended. Delegates to

ciation rate had reached a staggering one thirty-eighth of
e value. Then, in what was largely a knee-jerk reaction,
ongress made the decision to stop printing money com-
etely when the total reached $200 million—which would
appen in only a couple of months.

By the first quarter of 1780, the nation was mired in a desperate financial crisis. In February, Congress requested that
each state contribute $1.2 million monthly to the national
treasury. Some complied, but most did not because they could
not. And in March, when the inflation rate reached a wartime
high, Congress finally repudiated all the federal currency in
circulation, pricing it at only one fortieth of its face value.
With this action, the federal government essentially abrogated
its financial management responsibilities, wiped its financial
slate clean, and turned over nearly all public financial power to
the states. Unfortunately, this tactic would not work either.
And the situation only grew worse.

Through it all, George Washington, despite sending a
never-ending flow of letters to Congress, never really knew
when he was going to receive supplies or when he wasn't.
"One state will comply with a requisition," he wrote to a
friend, "another neglects to do it, a third executes it by halves,
and all differ in the manner, the matter, or so much in point
of time, that we are always working uphill."

Because he could not count on either Congress or the
states, Washington organized his own system of requisitioning
supplies. In 1780, for instance, he divided New Jersey into
eleven regions and assigned officers the responsibility of collecting grain and livestock from residents under the penalty of
force. Up to that point, he had avoided using his power to
seize supplies hoping instead that the governments would
come through. When that did not happen, he used the last resort of a leader—coercion. In addition, Washington had to
contend with an underground black market and profiteers
who stole supplies and then tried to sell them to the army at
exorbitant prices. "Hunt them down as the pests of society,"

Congress, bouncing between Philadelphia
napolis, and York, were frequently at odds a
the fledgling nation's financial crisis. Everyoi
knew how to manage affairs when it came to
reality, none of them had any experience with f.
let alone a national government. As a result, m
army could not be paid nor supplies ordered. Cor.
rency became virtually worthless, hard money wa
the government had no credit. Moreover, Congr
have the power to tax, and the states were alread
debt. So there was not only a lack of money, neither
an effective means to generate revenue.

Faced with such daunting problems, early in the
Continental Congress decided their only alternative
print paper currency. In 1775, they issued $6 million a
1776, another $20 million. However, the government d.
have the gold to back up the paper and, therefore, counte
the states to make good on it. But while many of the ind.
ual state legislatures did collect the notes as payment for ta.
they spent it rather than retire it. And in a further futile
tempt to ease their own financial worries, they followed tl
lead of Congress and began printing their own currency. Ove
the next several years, paper money was printed at increased
rates as the need for cold cash warranted. Of course, the value
of the currency quickly depreciated and inflation soared not
only because so much money was in circulation, but because
the public did not trust that the war could be won or the debt
redeemed.

In an effort to solve the problem, a number of futile, quick-
fix actions were taken. In 1777, for instance, Congress imposed rigid price regulations and wage controls that, in the
long run, were not able to hold up. In 1778, they declared
counterfeit some $40 million and offered to exchange it for
loan certificates. And in January 1779, the government can-
celed another printing of Continental bills and reissued $50
million in new notes as substitutes. But by November, the de-

he said in 1778. "No punishment is too great for the man who can build his greatness upon his country's ruin."

With Continental money soon to be taken out of circulation, help was needed immediately to mobilize Americans, and especially its representatives in Congress, to increase revenues to fund the war effort. Ideas were needed and, most importantly, action had to be taken.

That's when Thomas Paine again stepped forward to get the ball rolling and confront the issue head-on. On June 9, 1780, he published the ninth chapter of *The American Crisis*—and quickly followed it up with *The Crisis Extraordinary* (which related directly to America's financial emergency) in October. "The ability of any government," he wrote, "is nothing more than the abilities of individuals collected." Paine went on to propose specific "methods by which a sufficiency of money may be raised"—including citizen donations, taxation of the rich, a duty on imports, and securing loans from other nations. After putting forth his ideas, he then tried to persuade his readers of their worth. "It is not so much my intention," he wrote in *The Crisis Extraordinary*, "to propose particular plans for raising money, as it is to [show] the necessity and the advantages to be derived from it." And he closed out his essay by writing: "I have now waded through a tedious course of difficult business, and over an untrodden path. The subject on every point . . . was entangled with perplexities and enveloped in obscurity, yet such are the resources of America, that she wants nothing but system to insure success."

Subsequent to his publications, Paine then went out on foot and lobbied members of Congress specifically to seek more funds from France. And, on November 22, they finally relented and made a formal request of King Louis XVI for a loan of 25 million livres. The government also made several unsuccessful attempts to levy a five percent import duty, but could not obtain unanimous consent of the states. Early in 1781, Paine also traveled to Europe at his own expense in an effort to obtain more loans to finance the American cause. When it was all said and done, it was pretty well acknowledged that Thomas Paine's efforts successfully raised funds for the military and helped get inflation under control.

In the wake of Paine's writings, Congress also established a department of finance and approached Robert Morris, a wealthy and influential Philadelphia banker, to become the government's new superintendent of finances. Morris, however, demanded that certain conditions be met before he would accept the position. He wanted the power to appoint his own team, whoever they might be, and he insisted on total control of all fiscal matters relating to the government of the United States.

Even though the demands seemed outrageous, it was time to take some bold, unusual, and extraordinary steps. Because their previous efforts had been flawed by graft and incompetence, and due to the fact that the nation was in a desperate situation, Congress agreed to Morris's stipulations and, essentially, put the country's financial future in the hands of this one man.

Robert Morris was not an unknown quantity, though. He had been in Congress and had successfully led the Secret Committee of Trade. He was considered the best, most influential expert on finances in America—and he was, in truth, one of the few people who truly understood the intricacies and details of national finance. Within months, he set up an efficient system of bids and contract issuance, got the nation back on a hard currency standard, and established a financial team that was responsible to Congress for its actions. And, in May 1781, Congress accepted Morris's plan to create a national bank—which was the key initiative that turned the financial crisis into something entirely manageable. Eventually, the Bank of North America, during Morris's tenure, would lend the United States government more than $1.2 million.

The bold move of Congress, and the risk they took, turned out to be worth it in the long run. But many delegates felt it wasn't as big a gamble as some other representatives feared. They recalled that, back in 1776, Morris had demonstrated his worth and commitment to the cause when, after the battle of Trenton, George Washington appealed to him for help. With less than two days before most enlistments were to expire, the general had sent an urgent note to Philadelphia asking Morris to grant a loan to pay ten dollars to any soldier who reenlisted. "Every lover of his country must strain his credit," wrote Washington. "No time, my dear sir, is to be lost."

Without hesitating, Morris moved to action. He filled several bags with Spanish silver dollars, French half crowns, and English half shillings (rather than paper currency) and sent the money back to Washington with the rider who had brought the message—also promising to secure in gold and silver any other funds needed. In addition, Morris sent along a couple of barrels of wine for Washington and his officers to enjoy.

Shortly after assuming his new role as superintendent of finance, Morris was again called upon by George Washington—this time to finance the campaign at Yorktown. Again the banker rose to the challenge. He paid for the transportation and supplies needed to move the Continental Army to Virginia and also advanced the troops a month's salary. It was not generally known until many years later that Robert Morris had personally advanced more than $12,000 of his own money to make that happen. In addition, he would later guarantee with his own personal credit notes issued to the armed forces.

The financial crisis of the American Revolution could very easily have ended the war at any point in the conflict. And it very nearly did so on several occasions. After all, Great Britain was the strongest economic power on earth—and the colonies totally inexperienced in the complexities of major national and international finance.

Even though the founding fathers can be legitimately criticized for not having handled the finances of the new nation in a proper manner with fiduciary responsibility, they did eventually come to realize their shortcomings and turn it around. However, it should be remembered that most creative leaders do not naturally tend to enjoy the detailed complexities that often accompany financial matters. Most seem to be "wired" differently—preferring rather to dream the big dreams and set the grand goals. That is one reason why creative leaders who also enjoy and understand financial intricacies are so rare in proportion to the population—both in the eighteenth century and at the dawn of the twenty-first.

It is a leadership maxim that in every organization, especially those in business, financial matters must be well managed if the enterprise is to flourish. Accordingly, chief financial officers and competent budget directors are crucial to long-term success. The best leaders, therefore, surround themselves with experts in such matters, listen to them, and then act on their advice.

The founding fathers employed a variety of tactics in an effort to fix their financial crisis, nearly all of which failed miserably. When they finally admitted they could not fix it as a group, they turned to a member of the team who appeared to have the necessary skill and ability to solve the problem. And then they trusted that individual to do the right thing—delegating full responsibility and authority in allowing him to take the lead.

The mark of great leaders, whether they're founding a nation or running a business, is that they have an ability to delegate and trust people. Rather than order others to perform specific tasks, true leaders empower people to act on their own initiative to get the job done right.

It takes courage, patience, and a profound trust and respect for others in order to delegate effectively. It also takes follow-through. Leaders must necessarily transmit their grand vision and then step back and avoid excessive interference. Once a task is delegated, a fine line has to be walked—of sustaining and helping without taking over; of removing roadblocks and providing resources without usurping authority; and of observing from a distance while also being close at hand when guidance or advice is sought.

Moreover, the value of delegation in leadership is clear. It creates more time for the leader to act on other initiatives. It also allows experts in specific fields to provide solutions, thereby increasing the probability of success in any given endeavor. In general, the process of delegation permits greater achievement. Leaders, acting alone, cannot possibly do everything needed to accomplish the overarching vision. It only follows, then, that the larger an organization is, the more its leaders must delegate. Those leaders who do not have faith or trust enough in their people will end up attempting to do the entire job themselves. And such an occurrence almost always results in failure rather than success.

When France entered the war in 1778, Great Britain drastically shifted its military strategy. After three years of attempting to quell the rebellion in the northeast, the only thing they had to show for their efforts was the occupation of New York City. So, in an attempt to gain some new momentum, England's military leaders decided to shift the war southward away from Washington's main army and the center of American power in Philadelphia.

Accordingly, in the fall of 1778, the British launched a combined land and sea assault on Savannah, Georgia. The city finally fell on December 29 and, within a year, Great Britain was firmly in control of Georgia and started a move northward into the Carolinas. By April 1780, Generals Clinton and Cornwallis had led 14,000 naval and land troops to Charleston, completely surrounding the city and putting it under siege. The American forces there, led by General Benjamin Lincoln, at first refused to surrender and waged a noble fight. However, the British unleashed a brutal night-and-day artillery bombardment that threatened to destroy the city and all its inhabitants. On the twelfth of May, low on supplies and overwhelmingly outnumbered, General Lincoln surrendered his entire force of 4,000 men (including 2,500 soldiers of the Continental Army, 1,000 sailors, and 500 members of the militia).

For the Americans, the loss of Charleston was the largest surrender and the worst defeat of the American Revolution. As a result, the British now firmly controlled both Georgia and South Carolina and still held the city of New York. Moreover, General Clinton's massive military force would now head north and attempt to converge on America's center.

THE FOUNDING FATHERS ON LEADERSHIP

★ Remember that everyone thinks they know how to manage financial affairs, but few really can do it.

★ When you fail to receive help from your parent organization, don't just sit there. Create your own system to solve your needs.

★ Hunt down dishonest profiteers as the pests of society.

★ The ability of any organization is nothing more than the abilities of individuals collected.

★ When mired in a crisis, put forth ideas and then lobby to get them acted upon.

★ When you possess abundant resources, you should need nothing but system to insure success.

★ Every organization, especially those in business, must manage financial matters well if it is to be successful.

★ Surround yourself with experts in financial matters, listen to them, and then act on their advice.

★ When you cannot solve a problem with a group, turn to an expert member of the team and delegate full responsibility and authority to that individual.

★ The larger your organization, the more you must delegate.

"We fight, get beat, rise and fight again."

> General Nathanael Greene,
> 1780

"I trust the experience of error will enable us to act better in the future."

> George Washington, 1781

"I have not yet begun to fight."

> John Paul Jones, 1779

11 / *Refuse to Lose and Learn Continuously*

TEAM LEADERS
George Washington
Nathanael Greene
John Paul Jones

By mid-1780, after five years of war, neither the British nor the Americans seemed totally capable of winning the conflict outright. Even though the redcoats temporarily had the upper hand in the south and were pushing north, they could never really hope to beat the patriots on their home turf. On the other hand, George Washington's harassment strategy and his war of posts were beginning to wear thin. The troops were exhausted and becoming impatient, the governments (both federal and state) were in debt, and military victories were few and far between. For the founding fathers, winning the American Revolution increasingly became an issue of staying power and perseverance in the face of adversity.

In dealing with this problem, the commander in chief himself was clearly the leader of leaders. He was the one everybody else looked to when the going got toughest. And in what is perhaps his most enduring legacy, George Washington never gave up—and he never gave in.

In 1780, he and his army had to endure another desolate and desperate winter. This time more than 10,000 men were encamped at Jockey Hollow, a mountainous area near Morristown, New Jersey. The troops were short on food, clothing, and medical supplies; they hadn't been paid in months; and, climate-wise, it was by far the harshest winter of the war. Many of the men deserted, rebelled, or rioted—including a particularly threatening mutiny among troops from Massachusetts and Pennsylvania who were incensed over the terms of their enlistments.

There were also political attempts undertaken to usurp Washington's power and authority. The worst case occurred in the aftermath of the Americans' victory at Saratoga. General Horatio Gates, who had coveted the top spot for himself, conveyed news of his success directly to Congress, bypassing the commander in chief in the process. Saratoga stood out in stark contrast to recent defeats suffered by the main army at Brandywine and Germantown. Washington, who learned of Saratoga weeks later in a secondhand manner, was charged with listening to poor "counselors" and lacking initiative. Congress then appointed Gates president of the new Board of War and made General Thomas Conway, a Gates protégé, the new inspector general. It was Conway's controversial letter to Gates (now referred to as the Conway Cabal) that brought the entire issue to the attention of Washington and the rest of the army. All this occurred at the very time Washington was mired in his greatest crisis of the war—at Valley Forge.

In 1780, the Continental Army was further rocked by treason, this time with the defection of General Benedict Arnold to the British side. Arnold had been a hero at Saratoga and had fought valiantly for the American cause in both Canada and New York. But he was also a man of many paradoxes and conflicting personalities. Brash, arrogant, and somewhat paranoid, he felt that others had taken credit for his successes, and he became violently incensed at being passed over for promotion. On the other hand, he was a personal friend, protégé, and supporter of George Washington. So it came as a total shock when it was learned that Arnold had approached General Henry Clinton and offered his services to the Crown. For more than a year, he relayed detailed information of the American army's maneuvers to the British. Finally, a communiqué from Arnold was intercepted and it became known that he had demanded a huge sum of money in return for handing over the garrison at West Point. Washington later received a personal letter from Arnold confirming the treason. "Whom can we trust now?" said the general to an aide.

During the American Revolution, George Washington handled the adversity that goes with leadership by employing several different strategies. Let's briefly examine a few of his methods:

1. Continue to move forward.

First of all, it should be noted that George Washington never lost sight of his overall mission and did not allow himself to be distracted from taking necessary action to achieve that end. The Conway Cabal and all the controversy surrounding it occurred during the strife at Valley Forge, but it did not stop him from turning that negative situation into a positive outcome. Nor did the serious nature of the winter at Morristown in 1780 stop him from conferring with his generals to plan for the next major plans of the war. And the terrible personal trauma he suffered by the treason of Benedict Arnold did not prevent him from continuing to trust and confer with his other generals.

In essence, Washington's overriding commitment to achieving his goals took precedence over any short-term setbacks. As a matter of fact, that's exactly how he viewed such events—as setbacks, extraneous occurrences, or minor flies in the ointment—as compared to the all-important mission of achieving American independence. An unwavering commitment to this top priority prevented Washington from allowing his feelings to be hurt or from becoming too embroiled in such controversy. He simply did not have time for it.

2. Fight back.

Frequently, however, George Washington did fight back. From his quarters at Valley Forge, he sat down and wrote a series of pungent letters refuting the Conway Cabal, and with cold, clear, and precise reasoning, defended himself in the process. The offensive worked very well, as, in a relatively short period of time, General Conway wrote a letter of apology and eventually resigned his commission. Interestingly enough, Washington was quite magnanimous and free of ill will in his polite response to Conway. "My temper leads me to peace and harmony with all men," he wrote. "It is my wish to avoid any personal feuds or dissentions with those who are embarked in the same great national interest with myself, as every difference of this kind must in its consequences be very injurious."

In dealing with Benedict Arnold, Washington had raced to West Point only to learn that his former friend was previously informed that he had been exposed—and then fled by boat. The commander in chief quickly sent Alexander Hamilton on an expedition to try to capture the treasonous officer, but he got away again.

Washington also instituted a "get tough" policy with the

Massachusetts mutineers at Morristown by enacting strict discipline. But it was the sense of purpose he had worked hard to instill in the troops that ultimately quelled the uprising. When Henry Clinton learned of the mutiny, he sent two representatives to offer the mutineers money to join the British army. But the soldiers categorically refused the proposition, accepted terms offered by Congress, and then hanged the British agents as spies.

3. Be patient.

At Morristown in 1780, as at Valley Forge in 1778, General Washington penned endless letters to governors and governments appealing for supplies and support and then patiently waited for a response. "We have never experienced a like extremity at any period of the war," he wrote. "Unless some extraordinary and immediate exertions are made by the states from which we draw our supplies, there is every appearance that the army will infallibly disband in a fortnight."

In the wake of the Conway Cabal, Washington's friends and allies quickly rallied to his defense. In the army, Nathanael Greene, Alexander Hamilton, and virtually every other key general created a solid bloc of support and passionately articulated unbending devotion to their leader. When Gates approached General Daniel Morgan for help, Morgan's reply was swift and piercing: "Never mention that detestable subject to me again," he said, "for under no other man but George Washington will I ever serve." Lafayette categorically refused to have anything to do with Conway. In political circles, Sam Adams and John Adams jumped to Washington's defense— and Thomas Paine warned that no attempts to defame the nation's leader would escape his notice. Clearly, Washington's travels with the troops and personal relationship-building had paid off during this internal crisis.

And with time, Gates eventually cut his own throat by

showing his true colors. In June 1780, without consulting General Washington, Congress appointed him to command the army operating in the southern states. But within a few months, a monumental loss at Camden, South Carolina, would vividly demonstrate the difference between George Washington and Horatio Gates.

Leading up to the battle on August 16, the general was arrogant and overconfident. Even though he outnumbered the British by nearly two to one, he refused to listen to subordinates who told him he had only 4,100 troops as opposed to the more than 7,000 that he had personally calculated. On the eve of battle, he boasted to his men that he would dine "tomorrow in Camden with Lord Cornwallis at my table"—and then he issued the troops molasses and half-cooked meat that left them ill with upset stomachs on the day of the battle. Gates also made a major military blunder when he deployed his militias (rather than Continental regulars) at the center of action. When Cornwallis saw the mistake, he ordered a charge directly into the heart of the lesser-trained troops. The Americans immediately threw down their muskets and fled with the redcoats in hot pursuit.

Meanwhile, General Gates, who had positioned himself at the rear of the fighting, saw the massive retreat coming toward him, became frightened, and then panicked. Rather than riding to the sound of the guns and trying to rally his men into fighting positions as George Washington had done on several occasions, Horatio Gates grabbed a fast horse and galloped away in the opposite direction as fast as he could—leaving his troops without a leader. By nightfall, he was in Charlotte, some sixty miles away. But he didn't stop there. Three days later, Gates finally ended his personal retreat in Hillsboro, North Carolina—more than 180 miles from the battlefield in Camden, South Carolina. The clash, itself, was a complete British rout of the Americans. Gates lost all but 700 of his 4,100 men—and Cornwallis lost virtually none of his

2,000 troops. Afterward, severe criticism against Washington went away and Gates was never heard from again.

4. Learn from experiences and mistakes.

George Washington also learned from his past experiences and mistakes. For instance, where he had once hesitated to requisition supplies by force at Valley Forge, at Morristown there was no such vacillation. He quickly divided New Jersey into districts again and assigned a quota of grain and beef that each must furnish to the army. And as before when mutiny and disobedience threatened to disrupt morale and discipline, Washington instituted immediate punishments that included courts-martial, floggings, and house arrests. He had tried these methods before and they had worked—so he would continue to employ them in addition to new tactics gleaned from past trial and experience.

George Washington, similar to most great leaders, was a continuous learner. As the American Revolution progressed, he became more confident and improved at his job by assimilating his experiences, studying what he had done wrong— and then not making the same mistake twice. He reviewed the lessons of his loss at Long Island, looked at the tragic defeat at Germantown, and did a postmortem with his generals after Brandywine. After these military losses, Washington viewed them largely as lessons and experiences—not to dwell on or brood over, but to learn from. "I trust the experience of error will enable us to act better in the future," he stated in 1781.

The capacity and desire to learn continuously were traits common to nearly all the founding fathers, especially Adams, Jefferson, Franklin, Paine, and James Madison. As early as 1756, a youthful George Washington had said to his troops: "There ought to be a time appropriated to attain knowledge. Let us read." They were also prevailing attributes among the next tier of leaders with whom they surrounded themselves. The Marquis de Lafayette was a good example. When he first arrived at Valley Forge, General Washington apologized for the terrible condition of his army and the overall encampment. With all due humility, Lafayette replied: "I am here to learn, not to teach."

Moreover, learning was clearly a sentiment that was acted upon during the revolution after independence had been declared. Now that they had control over their own destiny and freedom to act on their own behalf (and on behalf of the people they represented), one of the first actions taken by the founding fathers was to promote education. Many of the new state constitutions, including those of Massachusetts, Pennsylvania, and Vermont, specifically mentioned a public responsibility to educate children. Georgia included a provision for the creation of a state university, and a number of new private universities were established in the northeast. The prevailing view of the period was eloquently expressed in 1781 by Thomas Jefferson in his publication *Notes on the State of Virginia*. "Every government degenerates when trusted to the rulers of the people alone," wrote Jefferson. "The people themselves therefore are its only safe depositories; and to render even them safe, their minds must be improved to a certain degree."

Learning and leadership go hand in hand; so much so, in fact, that a poor learner cannot possibly be a good leader. Harry Truman once perceptively noted that: "Not all readers can be leaders. But all leaders must be readers." More recently, modern leadership theory has emphasized the need for continuous learning. Stephen R. Covey, for example, wrote in *Principle-Centered Leadership* that: "principle-centered [leaders] seek training . . . to continually expand their competence, their ability to do things," and that "most of this learning and growth energy is self-initiated and feeds upon itself." Peter Senge, author of *The Fifth Discipline*, also emphasized the need for continuous learning—especially in the business world. "Leaders," he wrote, "are responsible for building organizations where people continually expand their capabilities to understand complexity, clarify vision, and improve shared mental models—that is, they are responsible for learning."

Leaders—especially those in a democracy—must know what it is that their people want and need. And in a technologically wondrous Information Age, as those wants and needs change with time, leaders must be *constant* learners—and *fast* learners at that, if they are to survive for long in a primary leadership role. In the twenty-first century, as in the first century, a leader's success—whether as a ship's captain or a head of state—will be determined by something as adroit as the simple formula: *Ability to Learn + Action = Effective Leadership.*

Future leaders would also do well to remember the comments of Mark Twain, who, in recalling his years as a riverboat captain on the Mississippi, wrote:

> Two things seemed pretty apparent to me. One was, that in order to be a pilot a man had to learn more than any one man ought to be allowed to know; and the other was, that he must learn it all over again in a different way every 24 hours.

While Samuel Clemens (a.k.a. Mark Twain) was one of the most famous riverboat captains of the nineteenth century, the greatest ship's captain of the American Revolution was a Scottish adventurer named John Paul—who added Jones to his surname in order to distance himself from a checkered past. In December 1775, he was commissioned a lieutenant in the newly formed Continental Navy. Almost immediately, Jones captured sixteen British merchant ships in the direct sea lane between London and the West Indies. Then he headed to the coasts of Nova Scotia where he took nine more enemy ships and destroyed key fisheries. Subsequently, in early 1777, Jones worked with Robert Morris to lay out and execute a daring plan to attack the British West Indies and key ports in Florida in hopes of luring the main enemy navy away from the east coast of the colonies.

By 1779, John Paul Jones (now a captain) was ordered to sail to France with the news of America's victory at Saratoga. Once there, he followed Benjamin Franklin's advice to sail up and down the English coastline and harass the enemy wherever he could. His "cruise" around the British Isles resulted in the capture of several ships, including the prized HMS *Drake* after a daring fight in the Irish Sea. Also that year, Jones took command of an old and rotting wooden-hulled ship, which he converted into a makeshift frigate and manned with a motley crew of inexperienced Americans. He named it the *Bonhomme Richard* in honor of Benjamin Franklin's Poor Richard pseudonym.

On September 23, as he sailed out to sea, Jones sighted forty British merchant ships under the protection of a brand new frigate, the *Serapis*, and a smaller ship, the *Countess of Scarborough*. HMS *Serapis* had all the latest innovations—a copper hull, double decking, and more than fifty cannons on board. Captain Jones and his men fearlessly sailed into the middle of the British fleet and attacked. The famous sea battle took place partly at night, was illuminated by the light of the moon, and lasted four hours in wave-tossed waters. Nearly two of those hours were spent exchanging cannonfire at point-blank range.

In the early going, it looked bad for the *Bonhomme Richard*. And when the captain of the *Serapis* shouted at the Americans to surrender, John Paul Jones is reported to have shook his fist and shouted back: "I have not yet begun to fight." In the end, clever maneuvering and a raging will carried the day. Jones lost about 150 of a crew that numbered only 300—and yet he still managed to force the captain of the *Serapis* to surrender. Moments later, the smaller *Countess of Scarborough* also struck its colors in defeat.

It was the greatest naval fight of the Revolution and John

Paul Jones had won a victory against overwhelming odds that would make him America's first and foremost American naval hero. A few months later, when the eighth chapter of *The American Crisis* was published, Thomas Paine (a personal friend of Jones's) wrote that "the expedition of Captain John Paul Jones" had finally placed the people of England in the position of "an endangered country"—and that they might now learn how it felt to be in America's position. Later, however, when Congress recommended Jones be promoted to the rank of rear admiral, the appointment was blocked by senior officers who were intensely jealous of his success.

But John Paul Jones dealt with jealousy as most great leaders did—he simply ignored the effect and plowed ahead with his mission. Most likely, Jones realized that jealousy is one of the most common emotions in human nature—and that people are always going to be envious of another's success or reputation. Moreover, it pervades all organizations—large or small. Due to the very nature of personal position, jealousy is ever present in leadership.

The most important attribute possessed by Jones was that—in the tradition of George Washington—he simply would not give up. It was not merely his naval skills or his commitment to the cause that made him successful. Rather, greatness for John Paul Jones rested in the fact that he absolutely refused to lose. His audacity, his daring, his risk-taking were the things that set him apart from the other naval officers—and they are the very qualities that caused them to be fiercely jealous of him. Moreover, this quality of perseverance in the face of overwhelming adversity—this courageous ability to fight back after being knocked down—again and again and again—was common to all the great leaders of the American Revolution.

It was especially true of General George Washington's right-hand man, Nathanael Greene, who, before the war, did not even have the military experience of a John Paul Jones. Greene was a wealthy and affluent Quaker from Rhode Island who managed his family's ironworks factory. He had asthma, walked with a limp, and overcame his lack of training by reading military manuals and studying the lives of great generals. And yet the thirty-three-year-old Greene—with high intelligence and piercing eyes—was a natural leader. On his own initiative, he organized his colony's three regiments of militia in preparation for war with England. And his commitment to the cause was unquestioned among other American leaders. In 1776, he wrote a letter of encouragement to Rhode Island's delegate to Congress, Samuel Ward: "The interests of mankind hang upon that truly worthy body of which you are a member," he told Ward. "You stand as the representatives not of America only, but of the whole world; the friends of liberty, and the supporters of the rights of human nature."

Washington took such an immediate liking to Greene upon their first meeting outside Boston in 1775 that the commander in chief soon designated him as his replacement if the need arose. And of course, Greene was at Washington's side for most of the next five years including Valley Forge and Trenton. Washington placed him in command of West Point in the wake of Benedict Arnold's treason and, earlier, had made him quartermaster general of the Continental Army. With his primary responsibility to secure food and supplies for the troops, Greene used literally every method within his means to achieve that end. He borrowed money from his good friends Robert Morris and the Marquis de Lafayette; he used the influence of Alexander Hamilton and other powerful leaders; and Greene also spent nearly all of his personal fortune to put clothes on the backs of his soldiers and food in their stomachs. "A fellow with nothing but a ragged shirt over his gaunt belly cannot fight well, no matter what his convictions," said Nathanael Greene to anyone who would listen. So he issued countless promissory notes to suppliers who readily accepted and cashed them. At the end of the war, Congress refused to reimburse Nathanael Greene and he went bankrupt.

In the wake of General Gates's retreat at the battle of Camden, Congress asked Washington to recommend a new commander for the southern armies. He immediately chose General Greene and, on October 7, 1780, Congress made the appointment official. Greene quickly left to assume his new command and, all along his ride south, he stopped to ask leaders in the various state governments to provide supplies—but he received little because there was nothing to give. Upon arrival, Greene wisely respected the culture of the armed forces already in place, consulting widely with the south's experienced officers. He embraced the guerrilla tactics of Francis Marion and Thomas Sumter because they worked so successfully, and also because the troops were not adequately trained to fight effectively against Cornwallis and his British regulars. Greene then placed a sizable portion of his army under the command of General Daniel Morgan, who subsequently won a brilliant victory at the Cowpens in South Carolina.

General Cornwallis soon became totally frustrated with the inability of his army to compete with the Americans. The British troops were bulky, slow-moving, and laden with bureaucratic procedures. He finally came to the conclusion that the only way he could beat the rebels was to start playing their game. Accordingly, in a bold move for an English general, Lord Cornwallis ordered most of the food, supplies, and excess baggage burned, and instructed his men to carry a limited amount of provisions on their backs. They were now going to be a quick-moving, turn-on-a-dime army that would be able to keep pace with the wily enemy—or so thought Cornwallis.

When word of the new British tactics reached Greene, he immediately reunited with Morgan's forces and began a rapid move north. As Cornwallis took off in hot pursuit, General Greene's only strategy was to stay ahead of the more numerous redcoats, cross several rivers and other difficult terrain, and hope to weaken their entire force. After all, the British were not used to fighting with American tactics, especially living off the land in the dead of winter.

Over a three-week time frame, Greene's men slogged through North Carolina, crossed the Yadkin and Deep rivers, and finally forded the Dan River into Virginia. On several occasions, Cornwallis almost caught the Americans. But with each week that passed, the British lost more and more men. Some died crossing the frozen rivers. Many were killed by Morgan and Greene's constant harassing raids. And others simply fell ill to the cold and miserable conditions.

When Greene crossed over into Virginia, he employed a lesson learned from General Washington by taking with him all the available boats so that Cornwallis could not follow. Once there, his experience as a quartermaster general came through. Greene had sent ahead for provisions to be waiting when he crossed the Dan, and there he rested for a few days to resupply and regenerate his weary troops. Cornwallis, on the other hand, had no such ability to resupply and, by this point, his men were equally weary. There was, however, one significant change in the situation as it existed three weeks prior—Nathanael Greene's forces, freshly replenished with new militia from Virginia and North Carolina, now actually outnumbered those of Cornwallis.

The British soon marched back to Hillsboro to rest. But just about the time they got there—in a scene reminiscent of Washington's maneuver at Trenton—Greene's troops were recrossing the Dan to attack Cornwallis. The American army constantly moved back and forth in an effort to confuse the redcoats, all the while nipping at their edges and harassing them.

On March 15, 1781, General Greene finally decided to engage Cornwallis in what he viewed as a favorable location—an isolated courthouse nestled in a forest. When the British regulars emerged from the woods into the small clearing, they were already tired from having just marched twelve miles that morning. So it could not have been a pleasant sight when they saw the entire American army lined up in formation to do combat.

During the battle, Greene employed General Morgan's tactic of having the militia out in front, firing two volleys, and then retreat behind more seasoned Continental regulars. He also followed Morgan's advice to place troops behind the militia who were ordered to shoot any man who did not fire a full two shots before they ran to the rear. The battle lasted for hours and was marked by fierce hand-to-hand fighting and one instance where Cornwallis actually ordered his artillery to fire into a massive melee that, in effect, killed both American and British troops. General Greene, seeing his men close to being overrun by the more seasoned redcoat regulars, finally gave the order to retreat.

The British remained in possession of the battlefield and claimed victory, but they paid an inordinately high price in losing more than 500 men (over one fourth of their army). American casualties were significantly lighter—only 250 out of about 4,000. When Cornwallis sent home a dispatch claiming a great victory at Guilford Courthouse, a British official commented that "another such victory would destroy the British army." Nathanael Greene, on the other hand, was optimistic: "The enemy got the ground the other day. They had the splendor, we the advantage."

A little over a month later, Greene's men again engaged the British at Hobkirk's Hill, North Carolina. But again, the more seasoned and disciplined redcoats—after suffering serious losses—forced the Americans back. Though ever in retreat, he would not admit defeat. "We fight, get beat, rise and fight again," wrote Nathanael Greene to a friend after yet another "official" military "loss." Indeed, from 1780 to 1781, this general lost five of six major battles with the British. But all the while, he fought with skill and imagination by employing the harassment tactics of George Washington. In the end, Nathanael Greene actually won the southern campaign and drove the British up to Yorktown, Virginia.

*   *   *

Nathanael Greene never conceded that he was whipped, nor did George Washington. And that was a pretty common denominator for all the founding fathers of the American Revolution. They all believed that if they refused to lose, if they did not admit to themselves that they were beaten—then they were, in fact, not beaten. There are literally dozens of examples of the great courage they displayed and the way they hung together to buck each other up.

One evening in Philadelphia, Thomas Paine was tripped, beaten, and thrown into a gutter by a small group who swore and yelled that they would "common sense" him. The writer took it in stride, though—viewing it as part of the price he had to pay for being in the lead.

In 1780, Benjamin Franklin wrote to George Washington to lift his spirits after a particularly brutal winter. "I must soon quit this scene," he stated in reference to his aging years. "But you may live to see our country flourish, as it will amazingly and rapidly after the war is over; like a field of young Indian corn, which long fair weather had enfeebled and discolored, and which in that weak state, by a thunder gust of violent wind, hail and rain, seemed to be threatened with absolute destruction; yet the storm being past, it recovers fresh verdure, shoots up with double vigor, and delights the eye, not of its owner only, but of every observing traveler."

And on June 4, 1781, British forces launched a surprise attack on the Virginia state legislature. Thomas Jefferson, having succeeded Patrick Henry as governor, was at Monticello (his home outside Charlottesville) conferring with several legislators when an express rider, John Jouett, showed up at sunrise to inform them that a mounted brigade was on the way. Jefferson immediately sent his wife and daughters (and the legislators) off to safety while he stayed behind to survey the situation through his telescope. Remaining until the last possible moment, when he observed the British troops ascending the trail toward him, Jefferson mounted a horse named Caractacus and headed off through the woods toward nearby Carter's Mountain.

The British troops had just missed capturing one of the most famous of the founding fathers. They stayed at Monticello for eighteen hours and were so impressed with the surroundings that orders were given to leave the estate as it was.

One can almost see Thomas Jefferson sitting atop Caractacus on Carter's Mountain—looking down as the British army occupied his home and property, waiting for them to leave.

It was, in a way, a metaphor for the entire war.

THE FOUNDING FATHERS ON LEADERSHIP

★ Never give up—and never give in.
★ Do not lose sight of your overall mission or be distracted from taking necessary action to achieve that end.
★ Fight back when attacked politically.
★ With time, political enemies will often show their true colors and cut their own throats.
★ Trust that the experience of error will enable you to act better in the future.
★ Appropriate a time to attain knowledge.
★ Upon starting a new assignment, tell everyone that you are there to learn, not to teach.
★ Remember that all leaders must be readers.
★ Ability to Learn + Action = Effective Leadership.
★ When confronted with jealousy, ignore it and plow ahead with your mission.
★ Upon arriving to assume a new leadership position, first respect the culture of the organization as it currently exists.
★ When outnumbered, stay a step ahead of the competition until they wear down and you outnumber them.
★ When you fight and get beaten, rise and fight again.

> "I am distressed beyond expression . . . for fear that the English fleet, by occupying the Chesapeake, may frustrate all our prospects. If you get anything new from any quarter, send it, I pray you, on the spur of speed for I am almost all impatience and anxiety."

> George Washington, to the Marquis de Lafayette, after taking the bold gamble to concentrate all his forces against Cornwallis at Yorktown, Virginia, August 1781

> "The play, sir, is over."

> Lafayette to Washington after the battle of Yorktown, October 1781

12 / Be a Risk-Taker

TEAM LEADER
George Washington

In early 1781, Bernardo de Gálvez, Spain's twenty-five-year-old governor of Florida and Louisiana, began a two-month siege of the British garrison at Pensacola, Florida. Spain had previously authorized de Gálvez to raid British outposts along the Mississippi River with a makeshift army of Spanish regulars, American militia, and native Indians. That campaign resulted in significant victories at Natchez, Baton Rouge, and Mobile. And when Pensacola finally fell, all of Florida came under Spanish control—effectively removing Great Britain's presence from the area.

While Americans were encouraged at Spain's entrance into the conflict, hopes for a favorable outcome to the war still looked exceedingly bleak. "Instead of having the prospect of a glorious offensive campaign before us," George Washington wrote in his diary, "we have a bewildered and gloomy defensive one, unless we receive a powerful aid of ships, land troops and money from our generous allies."

Despite private worries, America's leader maintained an outward optimism. And in an attempt to turn his hopefulness into action, he began planning a major campaign of harassment around the city of New York. His reasoning for implementing such a plan was simple: As long as the redcoats were in possession of a major American metropolis, it could be argued in Great Britain that the war effort was a viable endeavor. On a more personal level, though, Washington had never quite put behind him the sight of hundreds of English ships entering New York's harbor, the loss of the city, or being chased across the entire state of New Jersey. For the rest of the conflict, he would dream of the day the British would sail out of the harbor for good.

Washington's plan began to take root on May 21 when he met with the Comte de Rochambeau, commander of 6,000 French troops who were bivouacked in Newport, Rhode Island. Rochambeau, a fifty-five-year-old astute veteran of the Seven Years' War, spoke little English but cordially informed Washington through an interpreter that he had been directed by his government to place himself at the general's disposal. Together, the two leaders created a plan calling for joint action to seize British outposts in northern Manhattan. Both also agreed that their strategy should include a disruption of Britain's ability to freely move troops and supplies up and down the sea lanes along the Atlantic coast. Accordingly, Rochambeau sent a message to Admiral François de Grasse, commander of the French naval fleet in the West Indies, requesting that he sail for America as soon as time permitted. Rochambeau then began movement of his troops south and, by early July, he and Washington had hooked up in Connecticut and were creating detailed battle plans.

Meanwhile, in the southern campaign, Benedict Arnold showed up in a British uniform along with 1,200 other redcoats and began raiding American outposts along the James River in Virginia. When he reached Richmond, Arnold offered a deal to Governor Thomas Jefferson where he would spare the city if British troops were allowed to confiscate tobacco without resistance. When Jefferson refused, British General Arnold burned a large portion of the city and sent out an order to "get Jefferson." It was upon that command that Jefferson was nearly captured at Monticello.

Arnold's actions in Virginia branded him the archetypal traitor in American history. And his place was chiseled in granite when, upon his advice, British troops massacred the Americans at Fort Griswald, Connecticut, and then Arnold himself later landed an army near New London and proceeded to burn the town to the ground. Legend has it that Benedict Arnold stood in the tallest church belfry and watched with pleasure as the fire raged. It is also said that from there he could clearly see his birthplace, the town of Norwich, only twelve miles in the distance.

When an express rider reached George Washington with information of Arnold's attack on Richmond, Washington asked General Lafayette to lead an American force into Virginia to counter the British advance. Lafayette agreed and immediately marched overland with 1,200 men. In addition, Rochambeau committed to send another 1,200 French troops by sea to reinforce and join Lafayette.

Farther south, in North Carolina, Lord Cornwallis reevaluated his situation after the battle of Guilford Courthouse. Finding himself unable to successfully beat the Americans with their own physically draining harassment tactics, Cornwallis decided to withdraw and recuperate. Leaving their wounded behind, the redcoats then began a slow 200-mile

risking complete annihilation in one fell swoop? What would Washington do?

Lafayette, in command of some 3,500 men, quickly sent word to his commander that Cornwallis had settled along the coast at Yorktown with an exhausted army that numbered about 9,500. At virtually the same moment, Rochambeau received a letter from Admiral de Grasse stating that time constraints would not permit him to sail all the way to New York. Rather, he would sail directly to the Chesapeake Bay with his entire fleet, which included 3,000 troops and hundreds of cannon. Furthermore, he could stay only up until the beginning of October.

Washington immediately saw an opportunity. If he could surround Cornwallis by land, and de Grasse could control the sea lanes around Yorktown, there just might be a chance to secure a major victory and end the war. But it would be a big gamble for Washington, one fraught with many risks. Could he and Rochambeau move far enough south before Henry Clinton in New York found out what they were up to? Would Cornwallis still be at Yorktown when he got there? Would de Grasse arrive in the Chesapeake Bay before the British Royal Navy? Would there be favorable weather? At this point, the pivotal decision of the entire American Revolution was in the hands of one man.

George Washington decided to go for it.

First, he sent a confidential dispatch to Lafayette instructing him to keep Cornwallis bottled up at Yorktown until he got there. "I am distressed beyond expression . . . for fear that the English fleet, by occupying the Chesapeake, may frustrate all our prospects," he wrote. "If you get anything new from any quarter, send it, I pray you, on the spur of speed for I am almost all impatience and anxiety." Second, he placed half the Continental Army under the command of General William Heath with specific orders to keep Clinton in New York until it was too late for him to send reinforcements to Yorktown. Then, he persuaded the Comte de Rochambeau to move his

5,000-man army south to Virginia. And together, both men convinced French Admiral de Barras (who had transported Rochambeau to America) to take his fleet of ships (and 1,000 men) and sail for the Chesapeake to hook up with de Grasse.

Then, on August 19, Washington mobilized the Continental Army and began the nearly 500-mile march to Yorktown. He was embarking on a major offensive and, for the first time in the entire war, concentrating nearly all his strength in one place at one time. In so doing, George Washington was taking one of the biggest risks of his life. If he failed, America's independence could go right down the tubes. But if he could pull it off . . . Oh, if he could pull it off!

Washington immersed himself in the details of the entire operation. He personally oversaw the collection and distribution of food and supplies. He directed that roads and bridges be repaired ahead of his advancing troops. And he issued orders that all available boats be collected to aid in transportation across rivers and down the Chesapeake. After a long letter to General Benjamin Lincoln citing specific and detailed instructions for the march south, Washington signed his name and then added the following postscript: "The tow ropes [for] the boats ought to be strong [and] of sufficient length otherwise we shall be much plagued with them in the Bay and more than probably lose many of [the boats]."

As the combined forces began moving, the troops separated into three columns and took circuitous routes in an effort to confuse the British of their true destination. The entire movement was conducted with the strictest secrecy. None of the soldiers knew where they were headed until the last possible moment. General Washington was going to take no chances that word would leak back to Henry Clinton in New York. If that happened, and Clinton was able to mobilize, Washington might have to face all the British forces at Yorktown rather than only those led by Cornwallis. "Secrecy and dispatch must prove the soul of success to this enterprise," Washington told an aide. But, then again, the British commander would never have suspected such a move by Washington. After all, the Americans had been in their defensive posture for more than six years. There was really no reason for him to expect anything other than a few harassing raids on New York.

Along the way, most of the French and American forces passed through Philadelphia and, when they were within a few days' ride from Virginia, Washington rode ahead at a fast gallop to make a quick visit to his home at Mount Vernon. He had not been home in more than six years—not since he had left to assume command of the American forces on May 4, 1775. Upon arrival, his wife greeted him for the first time since Valley Forge—and there were several new grandchildren (born to his stepson and wife) he had never seen. But while it was good to be home, Washington still had a job to do. It was barely forty-eight hours before he was back on his horse heading for the main body of troops.

On September 5 an express rider dispatched by Lafayette reached General Washington where he was preparing for the water leg of his army's journey down to Yorktown. De Grasse, Lafayette reported, had arrived safely with his twenty-four ships of the line and six frigates. His 3,000 French troops had landed at Jamestown and were now part of Lafayette's army. De Grasse had control of Chesapeake Bay—and yes, Cornwallis was still bottled up at Yorktown.

An elated Washington turned back to meet Rochambeau's boat, which was due to land shortly at a nearby wharf. When the French commander and his staff arrived, they noticed the usually complacent and dignified American commander jumping up and down on the jetty like a small boy, waving his hat and a white handkerchief, grinning from ear to ear like a Cheshire cat. Rochambeau knew exactly what had happened—and he would never forget the moment.

Washington and Rochambeau would have been even more delighted had they known that, on that very same day, Admiral de Grasse had engaged in a two-hour battle with a slightly smaller British fleet. A portion of the Royal Navy stationed in the area under the command of Admiral Thomas Graves had headed to resupply Cornwallis and were astounded to find such a large French fleet already in possession of the Chesapeake Bay. Unable to defeat de Grasse, and unaware of the massive allied mobilization, Graves decided to sail his entire fleet back to New York. And, just four days later, French Admiral de Barras and his flotilla of ships arrived to join de Grasse, ensuring the complete entrapment of Cornwallis by both land and sea.

Upon his arrival in the Yorktown area, General Washington pitched the same weather-beaten tents he had used at Dorchester Heights in 1775. This time, however, he was in command of a powerful 20,000-man army fortified with hundreds of guns and seasoned artillerymen. And, just as he had done in Boston, he jumped on his horse and set out with several of his officers to personally survey the situation. When the group stopped under a clump of trees overlooking the enemy positions, British artillery spotters saw them and fired a couple of shots that exploded a few feet away. While the other officers rode to the rear, General Washington stayed his horse and kept peering through his telescope, seemingly unaware of the danger.

The American commander quickly realized that Cornwallis had not chosen a good location for his own defense. Yorktown was surrounded by rolling terrain that offered few military advantages, and without complete control of the sea, a proper defense was impossible. Cornwallis was trapped and outnumbered by more than a two-to-one ratio. Washington clearly knew that if he prepared carefully for the battle, there would be no way out for the British army.

The next step Washington took was to hold a council of war with, among others, Rochambeau and de Grasse aboard the French admiral's flagship. They agreed on a plan to completely encircle the British and implement a siege with heavy bombardment by both land and sea. At this meeting, the

American commander was also able to persuade the French admiral to stay in the area until at least the end of October. Back on solid ground, Washington ordered the digging of trenches and emplacement of redoubts; moved his artillery in place; and then divided the army into three divisions headed by Generals Lafayette, Benjamin Lincoln, and Baron von Steuben. Helplessly watching all the American movements, Lord Cornwallis penned a frantic letter that managed to get through to General Clinton in New York. "If you cannot relieve me very soon," said the desperate British commander, "you must be prepared for the worst."

Prior to beginning the assault, Washington invited every officer to visit him at a military reception. One witness recorded of the event: "Officers all pay their respects to the Commander-in-Chief. Those who are not personally known, their names are given by General Wayne. [Washington] takes every man by the hand. The officers all pass, receiving his salute and shake."

On October 9, General Washington was given the honor of firing the first cannon shot of the siege of Yorktown, thus beginning a furious bombardment from hundreds of guns. Over the next week, Lord Cornwallis tried a number of tactics to get out of his desperate situation. He sent squadrons out to try and take several American strong points and create a hole in which to escape but was unsuccessful. When he decided to ferry his troops across to Gloucester Point in an attempt to break through the enemy lines, a thunderstorm scuttled his plans. Nothing Cornwallis could do, or even think of, would extricate him from his hopeless position. After suffering heavy losses, he gave the order to have a drummer stand on a parapet and beat a signal for talks. One American officer wrote that all firing ceased and "I thought I had never heard a drum equal to it—the most delightful music to us all." Shortly thereafter, a British officer appeared with a white flag and was taken to see General Washington.

Cornwallis requested a twenty-four-hour truce to negotiate

terms. Washington granted him a two-hour cease-fire and demanded unconditional surrender. When the British commander agreed, Washington ordered all enemy arms and military equipment surrendered and all soldiers placed in captivity. Cornwallis and other British officers, decreed the American leader, would be paroled and provided with a ship.

Shortly thereafter, on October 19, 1781, allied forces assembled in a double line that strung out for more than a mile. The French, on one side, were splendidly dressed in neat white uniforms. The Americans, on the other, were still a rag-tag lot, clothed in patched breeches, shirts with holes in them, and an assortment of heavily worn garments. British redcoats, many of whom were either drunk or in tears, walked through the line and laid down their arms. Hessian troops did the same but were mostly stern and quiet.

George Washington and General Rochambeau, positioned at the head of the lines, were mounted on horses opposite each other. Lord Cornwallis, claiming to be ill, did not appear. And when General Charles O'Hara attempted to present Cornwallis's sword to Rochambeau the Frenchman directed him to Washington. But General Washington motioned him over to General Benjamin Lincoln, who had surrendered his own sword in the worst American loss of the war at Charleston. Lincoln triumphantly received the sword of surrender to cheers from the victorious Americans.

Shortly thereafter, Lafayette turned to George Washington. "The play, sir, is over," he said. Washington smiled and then headed back to his tent to compose a dispatch to his superiors. "I have the honor to inform Congress," he wrote, "that a reduction of the British Army under the command of Lord Cornwallis, is most happily effected. . . ."

When word of Washington's victory at Yorktown reached London more than a month later, the reaction of Britain's prime minister, Lord Frederick North, pretty much summed up the situation. "Oh, God!" he exclaimed. "It is all over."

*   *   *

When Cornwallis withdrew to Yorktown, he wanted to rest and be resupplied—and he thought he had more than enough troops so as not to be bothered by the enemy. Ironically, the British had Washington in worse positions several times during the previous six years of war. For instance, in 1778, when what was left of the Continental Army holed up at Valley Forge, General Washington's strategy was to rest, rebuild, and renew his weary troops. Had the British attacked at that moment, they would have ended the American Revolution with a great victory. But unlike Washington at Yorktown, the British leadership preferred to take no risks. Instead, they opted to nestle in Philadelphia for the winter, in warm, comfortable surroundings.

Yorktown was George Washington's one great moment in time. He seized on the opportunity to completely reverse the British and American roles. At that instant, Washington creatively concentrated nearly all of his forces—and risked everything he had—for one shot at victory. Moreover, he employed several key leadership techniques: He utilized the fruits of the *alliances* that had been built with the French; he effectively employed *diversity* to his advantage; he cleverly *leveraged his resources*; he was *flexible* enough to change his plans quickly when a great opportunity unexpectedly presented itself; and he took a bold and *courageous risk*.

Had Washington been any less of a leader, had he played it safe, the war could have gone on for years, perhaps until some sort of compromise was reached. In the end, when it came right down to it, the American leadership took the risk and won—and the British leadership played it safe and lost.

In general, people admire the risk-taker, but hesitate at taking any risks themselves. The same is true for change itself. Most people love the *idea* of change, but naturally resist even the slightest alteration in their daily lives. Howard Gardner, in *Leading Minds*, noted than "exemplary leaders" display "an inclination from early childhood for risk-taking . . . in order to achieve their ends," and that "leaders are risk-takers [who] do not easily withdraw from the fray." Moreover, when such a rare individual demonstrates a disposition toward change, it implies there is also a willingness to take risks.

It is completely understandable, therefore, that risk-taking is a common trait among great leaders. By their very nature, those who lead must be willing to take enormous chances. If they are to take people to places they have not yet been, they must be willing to accept the natural human behavior that accompanies the change process. And history has clearly demonstrated that such human reactions against a leader can involve slander, defamation of character, removal from positions of power and authority, physical attacks, and even murder.

In that context, the courage to introduce sweeping changes, to try new and innovative things, can be construed to be an ultimate example of risk-taking. Leaders are, in effect, change agents. They encourage others to take risks and, if they fail, the leader does not place blame, but rather, urges them to try again. The next attempt may achieve a favorable outcome.

History's best-known heroes were leaders who realized that the greater the risk, the greater the glory. And few ever achieved a more far-reaching victory than George Washington did at Yorktown—as that was the battle that effectively ended the American Revolution, which, in turn, led to the formation of the first truly free and democratic government in human history.

THE FOUNDING FATHERS ON LEADERSHIP

★ Even though you may have private worries, maintain an outward optimism and hopefulness.

★ Even with a series of defeats, you may be victorious in the long run.

★ Keep your eyes and ears open for the time you may have finally turned the tables on the competition.

★ Have the courage to seize your one moment in time.

★ When undertaking a crucial endeavor, immerse yourself in the details of the operation.

★ When you have a clear advantage, prepare your next moves carefully.

★ Before a major action, meet all the members of your team personally. Shake their hands and salute their efforts.

★ Those who lead must be willing to take chances.

★ Remember that, as a leader, you must be willing and prepared to accept the negative human behavior that accompanies the change process.

★ Encourage others to take risks. When they fail, urge them to try again.

★ As a leader, you are an agent of change.

★ The greater the risk, the greater the glory.

PART IV
AFTER THE REVOLUTION

"We must make the best of mankind as they are, since we cannot have them as we wish."

George Washington, 1776

"I am afraid that Congress, viewing this stroke at Yorktown in too favorable a light, may think our work too nearly closed, and will fall into a state of languor and relaxation."

George Washington, to
General Nathanael Greene,
November 1782

13 / *Understand Human Nature*

TEAM LEADER
George Washington

For the most part, the final outcome of the American Revolution was determined after the battle of Yorktown. And with the exception of a few minor skirmishes, all battlefield fighting ceased.

In London, King George III could no longer generate any support in a Parliament where the vast majority of delegates were demanding peace. On March 20, 1782, direction of the British government took a dramatic turn as the ministry of Lord North fell and the Marquis of Rockingham agreed to become prime minister on the condition that America's independence be recognized. That same month the House of Commons passed a resolution that labeled all those who continued a war against America enemies of Great Britain. An order was also issued to evacuate British troops at Charleston and Savannah "in consequence of an unsuccessful war." A major British presence, however, was maintained in New York City.

The government then dispatched an envoy to Paris to initiate informal peace negotiations with Benjamin Franklin. But just as the talks were beginning, the Marquis of Rockingham died suddenly and the secretary of state, Lord Shelburne, became prime minister. As a result, Great Britain's already feeble leverage in the peace process was even more weakened.

Meanwhile, the United States Congress formally nominated Franklin, John Adams (presently at The Hague in the Netherlands), and John Jay (then minister to Spain) to negotiate details of the peace with Great Britain. Thomas Jefferson was also nominated, but declined service due to his wife's illness. The committee was then instructed by Congress to secure independence as a primary goal—and to use its discretion on all other issues. Subsequently, formal peace talks began in Paris on October 1782—a full year after the American victory at Yorktown.

Now, one might think that after Washington's stunning success the war would have come to a swift conclusion; that Great Britain would leave American shores; that the United States would begin its climb to greatness; that members of the American military would be hailed as heroes in their own land; and that the individual states would band together— having realized that it was only through their combined unity and teamwork that they were able to achieve such a great outcome to the American Revolution.

Well, not so fast. Human nature got in the way.

There were, in fact, many new problems created by winning the war. Six years of revolution had required a vision and goals aimed specifically at achieving victory. But now that the war was won, and the original mission accomplished, everything changed. Strategic plans that only a few years ago seemed bril-

After his statement, the officers disbanded and the crisis eased. But while George Washington managed to quell the uprising resulting from the Newburgh Addresses, it was not the only such mini-rebellion he had to put down in the wake of victory. The previous summer Colonel Lewis Nicola, stationed at West Point, approached the commander in chief with a suggestion that the government be seized by force and converted to a monarchy with George Washington as king. Washington, though, immediately fired off an angry and biting letter rejecting the proposal outright. "I must view [your suggestion] with abhorrence and reprehend it with severity," he wrote to Nicola. "If you have any regard for your country—concern for yourself or posterity—or respect for me, [then] banish these thoughts from your mind, and never communicate a [similar] sentiment of like nature."

And, in what may have been the most terrifying of the internal mini-rebellions, the Philadelphia State House where Congress was holding an emergency session was surrounded by 400 armed and mutinous Pennsylvania soldiers who demanded their back pay. The spooked delegates quickly adjourned to Princeton, New Jersey, where they could be closer to Washington's cloak of protection. After that episode, though, the Congress never returned to Philadelphia, opting the next year to move to Annapolis, Maryland.

In the wake of the Newburgh conspiracy and the Pennsylvania troop uprising, Congress eventually approved a plan to grant the nation's soldiers full pay for five years. But still there were virtually no funds to make the plan work. As an alternative, the government issued federal securities and promissory notes to the veterans, none of which were honored by banks and were laughed at by businessmen in the various states.

By the summer of 1783, Congress and Washington had furloughed nearly all of the enlisted men of the United States Continental Army. But the undeniable truth remains that the tens of thousands of men who fought to win America's independence were not paid what was owed them by the federal government—nor were they treated much like great heroes by their country after the fighting had stopped.

Rather, Americans everywhere turned their primary attention to rebuilding the economy. The middle Atlantic states (Delaware, New York, New Jersey, and Pennsylvania) led the charge with the processing of agricultural products and manufactured goods. In New England, the fishing and whale oil industries began to take off again. And southern states struggled to build back their agricultural base of rice, corn, wheat, and tobacco. Moreover, shipping and overseas trade picked up rather quickly as markets began to open in the French West Indies, the Netherlands, Spain, and Portugal.

But while inflation and consumer prices began to drop in most of the country, government finances remained in a dour state of affairs. Hard currency flowing out of the country to pay for an overwhelming trade deficit combined with the large national debt to create a mediocre economic recovery and depressed trade. Slow progress then caused many Americans to question the intelligence and competence of their leaders. In general, people began to feel that either the founding fathers had not completely thought through the concept of independence—or that something was terribly wrong with the current system of government.

In truth, the Articles of Confederation, perhaps suitable in wartime, proved less than perfect in the context of peacetime. The Articles, which were finally ratified and took effect on March 1, 1781 (only six months before Yorktown), collectively created the first constitution of the United States of America. But it was a flawed document in many ways. Congress, for example, became a relatively weak government body—without the power to tax; with no way to enforce its actions; and without the power to regulate commerce and industry. Nor did the Articles provide for a chief executive or a national judiciary. Rather, it specifically mandated that each state was to "retain its sovereignty, freedom and independence, and every power, jurisdiction and right." The states, then, citing their rights under the Articles of Confederation, consistently refused to support any plan that would involve taxing their own citizens. And, as a result, the delegates to the national Congress were forever in fear of offending any state legislature—for the slightest offense might result in secession from the union.

But for all the constraints imposed upon it by the Articles of Confederation, Congress did manage to make some great strides in providing for the growth of the republic. Over the several years immediately following the Revolution, for instance, the delegates to Congress managed to arrange for the settlement and governance of the western territories. The fact that they were able to achieve anything at all was remarkable given the rush by other nations and the individual states to seize the lands as their own. The Spanish, who controlled Florida, Louisiana, and the west bank of the Mississippi River, began maneuvering to gain control of land east of the Mississippi to the Appalachian Mountains—especially Kentucky and Tennessee. And states such as Connecticut, North and South Carolina, Georgia, Massachusetts, New York, and Virginia all claimed parts of the western territory as their own. Veterans groups also demanded that the lands be given to them as due payment and reward for their service.

At this crucial moment, however, Thomas Jefferson stepped back into the picture and convinced his home state to cede territory it claimed (under seventeenth-century charters) northwest of the Ohio River over to the United States government. Jefferson was then appointed by Congress to create a process for development of the western lands. He followed up by suggesting that new states be established from all the territories; and that after a period of temporary territorial government they be admitted to the union on equal footing with the thirteen original colonies.

Thomas Jefferson also favored giving away property to veterans and other settlers, but Congress felt that the heavy burden of the national debt would not allow it. As a result, the

Ordinance of 1785 was enacted, stipulating that land was to be divided into six-square-mile townships (each township consisting of thirty-six one-mile-square sections). After surveying, the property would be sold at auction. And in an effort to provide for the future, Congress reserved four sections in each township for the federal government. Section 16 would be reserved specifically for the emplacement of public schools. Congress further stipulated that all land sales "shall be applied to the burgeoning national debt . . . and to no other purpose whatsoever."

The Ordinance of 1785 was a precursor to the more famous Northwest Ordinance (enacted two years later) where Congress laid out specific methods for new states to be admitted to the confederation on an equal basis. America's leaders, such as George Mason of Virginia, were astute enough to realize that Congress had to provide a fair and equal chance for all—or else there would be trouble. "[Westerners] will have the same pride and other passions which we have, and will either not unite with or will speedily revolt from the Union, if they are not in all respects placed on an equal footing with their brethren."

It was with such insights into human nature that the founding fathers were able not only to prepare for and win the American Revolution—but were able to deal with the turbulent and traumatic years that followed. After the fighting stopped, there was chaos, indecision, uncertainty, and apprehension. At that point, the nation needed effective leadership more than ever.

The founding fathers clearly understood that it was much easier to inspire movement of the masses during a crisis situation. But after a war is won, a tendency sets in among people to become somewhat complacent. "I am afraid Congress, viewing this stroke at Yorktown in too favorable a light," wrote George Washington to Nathanael Greene in 1782, "may think our work too nearly closed, and will fall into a state of languor and relaxation."

Washington also realized that a transitionary period can be much more dangerous and traumatic than war itself. "In times of turbulence," he remarked only two years before his death, "when the passions are afloat, calm reason is swallowed up in the extremes to which measures are attempted to be carried. The man who acts from principle, who pursues the paths of truth, moderation and justice, will regain his influence."

The founding fathers were leaders who thought deeply about human nature—about what motivated others, how people reacted in different situations, how their thought processes worked in various situations, and about how factions and extremist points of view manifested themselves. Consequently, they realized that rivals or competitors will almost always attempt to take advantage of a perceived weakness—such as attempts to seize property and assets from both the victors and the defeated following a major crisis. "Wherever there is an interest and power to do wrong, wrong will generally be done," wrote James Madison after the revolution. "[Democracy's] principles are as easily destroyed, as human nature is corrupted. . . ." said John Adams in 1776. And Washington, who perhaps thought more about human nature than most, realized that "men are very apt to run into extremes" and that "hatred may carry some into an excess." "We must make the best of mankind as they are," he later wrote, "since we cannot have them as we wish."

For every period of great transition, and for changing times in general, new leadership is required—with new ideas; fresh, imaginative, innovative, creative ideas—around which people can mobilize and rally. An overarching vision or mission must be created—and that vision must be transferred to the masses of people—through involvement, persuasion, and inspiration.

Without effective leadership, human nature is such that people will withdraw into their own world and create their own group of dissidents. There is an unwillingness to accept new situations or to act quickly. A conservative approach is more common (and often more natural) than a liberal one.

People are more likely to stick with the old ways, to not try new things until they're absolutely certain, absolutely convinced that they should act—and then action is taken only precipitously and tentatively. "The nature of man is such that we must feel ourselves before we can think," observed Washington in 1797.

An underlying premise of leadership, therefore, is to unite separate factions and mobilize them toward a common end. Essentially, the entire process of change should be repeated at regular intervals. And leaders, as agents of change, must understand human nature if they are to move large numbers of people down the same path—toward a new destination.

In general, there are two overarching reasons why leaders must have a good understanding of human nature:

1. To understand the motives and reactions of the people they lead.

This principle involves such simple points of human nature as a person's negative reaction at being told what to do rather than being asked his or her opinion. By understanding what makes people tick, leaders will be better prepared for the reactions they will experience from followers. Accordingly, they'll be better able to implement the changes they desire.

Those who do not understand human nature may find themselves in a similar situation to the one in which the editor of the *California Star* newspaper found himself when a rumor reached town in 1848 that gold had been discovered at Sutter's Mill. Author John McPhee related the incident in *Assembling California:*

> In an April memorandum, the editor of the *California Star* says, in large letters, "HUMBUG" to the idea that gold in any quantity lies in the Sierra. Six weeks later, the *Star* ceases publication, be-

cause there is no one left in the shop to print it. . . . [In San Francisco] ministers have abandoned their churches, teachers their students, lawyers their victims. Shops are closed. Jobs of all kinds have been left unfinished.

2. To improve themselves by effectively interacting with others.

Leaders must also understand human nature so that they may better understand themselves. By having an awareness of why people behave the way they do, a good leader will be able to apply that knowledge to his or her own specific performance and interactions. The most frequent result of such self-analysis causes the leader to become more compassionate and more empathic. When leaders display such tendencies toward followers, it almost always results in greater acceptance and genuine affection for the leader.

This fundamental notion, however, is certainly not a new idea. It was clearly noted several thousand years ago in this Taoist story of ancient China:

> When Yen Ho was about to take up his duties as tutor to the heir Fo Ling, Duke of Wei, he went to Ch'u Po Yu for advice. "I have to deal," he said, "with a man of depraved and murderous disposition. . . . How is one to deal with a man of this sort?" "I am glad," said Ch'u Po Yu, "that you asked this question. . . . The first thing you must do is not to improve him, but to improve yourself."

*　　*　　*

In what turned out to be one of the greatest diplomatic efforts in world history, Benjamin Franklin, John Adams, and

John Jay negotiated the 1783 Treaty of Paris that formally ended the American Revolution. Several European nations (Spain and Russia, among others) sought to crash the party and mediate proceedings, but the American delegation steadfastly blocked any attempts at outside influence. While Great Britain initially attempted to keep possession of Charleston, Savannah, New York City, Maine, and large portions of the northwest territories, Franklin refused. He then countered with the audacious proposal that all of Canada be ceded to the United States. In the end, America achieved its primary goal of unchallenged independence—plus another series of secondary objectives, including: new boundaries, access to international waterways, free trade and navigation along the Mississippi River, and the total evacuation of British forces from United States territory. King George III formally proclaimed an end to hostilities on February 4, 1783. And on April 15, the United States Congress ratified the Treaty of Paris and declared the war over.

A few months later, upon hearing that Thomas Paine had contracted scarlet fever, George Washington traveled to Prince Town, New Jersey, to visit and lift the spirits of his friend. He stayed for three weeks as Paine convalesced. The two men spent nearly the entire time together chatting, joking, and sharing memories of the prior eight years of conflict. When Paine's overcoat was stolen, Washington handed over his own and insisted it be accepted. Thomas Paine then wore George Washington's overcoat for years afterward.

During that visit, the commander in chief received word that the British occupying forces stationed in New York would finally leave American shores. Paine, by then almost completely recovered, rode with General Washington to New York City to witness the event. They arrived just as the last of the British vessels were leaving the docks. George Washington's mind must have wandered back to Long Island and Trenton when the British arrived just in time to see the last of his troops fleeing across the East River and the Delaware.

Now he had arrived just in the nick of time to see the very thing he had been dreaming about for eight drawn-out years—the last of the British troops floating out of the harbor, out into the Atlantic, out of the United States for good. The tyrants were gone, gone at long last. And later that day, November 25, 1783, Washington and Paine rode on horseback at the head of a huge parade—through city streets that were lined with thousands of cheering American citizens—*free* American citizens, *free* at long last.

George Washington next sat down and wrote a letter to Congress informing them of the events of that day. He then began immediate preparations to leave the military service, deciding to travel to Annapolis to speak personally with members of Congress and formally resign his commission. Then he would head home to Mount Vernon on the Potomac.

Upon the general's departure on December 4, thirty senior officers gathered at Fraunces Tavern in New York to say goodbye. When Washington entered the room, there was a "breathless silence," as one witness recorded. Tears welled up in everyone's eyes. No one could speak. Finally, the general interrupted the stillness by filling his wine glass and motioning for everyone else to do the same. "Gentlemen," he said lifting his glass in a toast, "with a heart full of love and gratitude, I now take leave of you. I most devoutly wish that your latter days may be as prosperous and happy as your former ones have been glorious and honorable."

After everyone sipped their wine, Washington, with a quiver in his voice, said: "I shall feel obliged if each of you will come and take me by the hand." One by one, the officers approached and shook their leader's hand. Many embraced and kissed him with sobs of affection. No one spoke a word. There were no words appropriate enough for the moment. But every man knew what the other was feeling and thinking. Every man knew. General Washington then stepped quietly out of the tavern, walked down to the docks, and boarded a barge that was waiting to ferry him across the Hudson.

On December 23, 1783, he stood before Congress and offered his formal resignation as commander in chief of the Continental Army of the United States of America. Rising slowly when introduced, he read his prepared remarks. Several delegates noticed that his hand trembled throughout the three-minute speech. Washington bowed to the Congress and offered "my sincere congratulations" on securing independence. He thanked all Americans for their generous support and praised and commended the officers and soldiers who fought for freedom. "I should do injustice not to acknowledge the services and merits of the gentlemen who have been attached to my person during the war," he said. And then Washington concluded his brief remarks: "Having now finished the work assigned me, I retire from the great theater of action, and, bidding an affectionate farewell to this august body under whose orders I have so long acted, I here offer my commission, and take my leave of all the employments of public life."

After shaking hands with many members of Congress, George Washington, private citizen, then mounted his horse and rode home alone. He arrived at Mount Vernon just before sunset on Christmas eve. His wife, Martha, was standing in the driveway to greet him.

On the eighth anniversary of the battles of Lexington and Concord, Thomas Paine published *The Last Crisis, No. XIII.* "The times that tried men's souls are over," he wrote. "I have followed [the war] from beginning to end, through all its turns and windings. [The] cause was good, the principles just."

THE FOUNDING FATHERS ON LEADERSHIP

★ New problems are often created after a revolution is won.

★ After a common enemy has been vanquished, or an overarching mission achieved, members of the organization often exhibit a tendency toward isolationism.

★ Once people slip into an isolationist mode, they often become jealous and suspicious of each other.

★ In the wake of victory, be prepared to put down many mini-rebellions.

★ Slow progress toward economic prosperity causes members of the organization to question the intelligence and competence of their leaders.

★ It is much easier to inspire movement of the masses during a crisis situation than in a time of relative peace.

★ A period of transition can be more dangerous and turbulent than war itself.

★ Remember that whenever there is an interest and power to do wrong, wrong will generally be done.

★ Take the best of people as they are, since you cannot have them as you wish.

★ Changing times require new approaches and new ideas.

★ Understanding human nature not only allows you to comprehend the motives and reactions of the people you lead, it also helps you improve yourself.

★ There never was a good war or a bad peace.

"[We] now have a national character to establish, [and must] form a constitution that will give consistency, stability, and dignity to the union."

George Washington,
April 1783

"We the people of the United States, in order to form a more perfect union, establish justice, insure domestic tranquillity, provide for the common defense, promote the general welfare, and secure the blessings of liberty to ourselves and our posterity, do ordain and establish this Constitution for the United States of America."

Preamble to the Constitution,
September 17, 1787

14 / Compromise and Create the Culture

TEAM LEADERS
James Madison
Alexander Hamilton
Benjamin Franklin
George Washington

In the half decade following Yorktown, America was a young country sowing its wild oats. Like a group of small children who had been stuck in a car for an all-day drive, once the long ride was over Americans began running around expending all their pent-up energy. Citizens pounded their chests and shouted aloud their independence for all to hear. Bragging rights had been earned by beating the number one power in the world. The new nation—now bustling with renewed activity, fresh ideas, and original thinking—was on the brink of bursting onto the world scene as a leader in both industrial and scientific thought. "We are making experiments," Benjamin Franklin astutely observed.

At the same time, however, the nation was still recovering from years of personal sacrifice and war. A rebellious spirit still existed and sometimes manifested itself in ways that were detrimental to the progress of the country. In 1786, for example, when the Massachusetts state legislature increased taxes on its citizens in an effort to meet the federal government's request for funds, debt-ridden farmers in the western part of the state armed themselves and attacked local municipal courts in an attempt to prevent farm foreclosures. The mini-rebellion, led by activist farmer Daniel Shays, had to be quelled by the Massachusetts militia (which was supported by private funding from wealthy businessmen in the more populous and more urban eastern portion of the state). The most disturbing aspect of Shays's Rebellion was the fact that the men who took part in it were not members of some extremist group. Rather, they were respectable, upstanding citizens driven to an act of desperation in order to survive. And to make matters worse, most of the farmers were veterans of the American Revolution.

With such serious events happening, it did not take a genius to figure out that the new system of government was simply not working well. Accordingly, a major political struggle steadily grew between those who espoused states' rights and a loose national confederation—and those who favored a strong centralized federal government. Intense political debate raged between these two factions for years. Newspapers and pamphlets were produced on a weekly basis extolling the virtues—and the grim predictions—of both points of view.

But people just could not seem to agree on any single method of governance after the battlefield fighting had ceased. Americans, at that point, were living with the terrible struggle that had been foreseen in 1776 by John Adams. "I have ever thought it the most difficult and dangerous part of the business Americans have to do in this mighty contest," he wrote in anticipation of future independence, "to contrive some method for the Colonies to glide insensibly from under the old government into a peaceable and contented submission to new ones."

In general, the new political struggle stimulated intense discussion among the nation's leaders. And many of the founding fathers began writing a flurry of letters back and forth to each other—letters that expressed concern for the future of the fledgling nation they had just helped to create.

From Mount Vernon, George Washington fretted about the future. "We are either a united people under one head, for federal purposes," he wrote, "or we are thirteen independent sovereignties, eternally counteracting each other." To Lafayette in France, he stated that "we are placed among the nations of the earth and now have a national character to establish," and that the people must "form a constitution that will give consistency, stability, and dignity to the union."

Clearly, the development of America was at a turning point. Something needed to be done. A new, more effective culture had to be created and established. But who would do it—and how would it happen?

It was precisely at this moment in time that several leaders stepped forward to assume responsibility for the task at hand. They were two new leaders with passionate commitment and specific expertise suited to the task—and two older leaders with an intimate history of the past struggle. It was to be a perfect combination of the past and the present combining to build a bridge to the future.

The two new faces were James Madison and Alexander Hamilton. Both were relatively young men. Madison, from Virginia, was thirty-six; Hamilton, from New York, thirty. Both were diminutive in size. Hamilton, often called the "Little Lion," was five feet seven inches while Madison, a thin five feet four inches and barely one hundred pounds, was described by one of his contemporaries as "no bigger than half a piece of soap." Madison had earned a solid reputation as a delegate to Congress for many years. He had also emerged the leader of a potentially contentious meeting of commissioners at Mount Vernon in 1785 where a series of compromises were worked out between Maryland and Virginia regarding navigation rights to the Potomac River and Chesapeake Bay. Hamilton, during the war, had been a captain of artillery at Trenton and Yorktown as well as aide-de-camp to General Washington.

After the Revolution, both men had persistently lobbied for a strong central government. Both, for instance, were delegates to the Annapolis Convention of 1786, which was convened to consider how to bring the states together for "common interest and permanent harmony." Unfortunately, only five states sent representatives and the meeting was short-lived. Madison and Hamilton, however, attempted to turn the unsuccessful event into a clarion call for action. They worked together to architect a final report issued by the Annapolis Convention suggesting that all the states meet in May 1787 to, in Hamilton's own words, "take into consideration the situation of the United States, to devise such further provisions as shall appear to them necessary to render the constitution of the federal government adequate" to solve the current crisis. Because of the impact of Shays's Rebellion and other serious problems, America's leaders clearly understood that change was needed. And when Congress, on February 21, 1787, approved a resolution in favor of just such a meeting in Philadelphia, Madison and Hamilton got their wish.

Benjamin Franklin had returned to America in the autumn of 1775. Now eighty-one years old and in frail health, the old gentleman kept pretty much to himself at his home in Philadelphia. Nevertheless, he was unanimously selected as his state's nominee to the Constitutional Convention, which was set to be held only a few blocks away from his house.

The gathering was set to begin on May 14, 1787, but a quorum could not be mustered for another eleven days. Meanwhile, on May 13, George Washington (chosen as a delegate from Virginia) arrived on horseback and drew large crowds as he was instantly recognized by Philadelphians in the streets. He rode directly to the home of his friend (and financier of the Revolution) Robert Morris, where he resided for the next four months while Congress was in session. After stowing his gear and settling in a bit, Washington called on Ben Franklin later that same day to pay his respects and to discuss the upcoming convention. These were the two seasoned leaders who, along with James Madison and Alexander Hamilton, would have the most impact on the outcome of the future Constitutional Convention.

During breaks over the course of the proceedings, Washington also took time out to visit his former home away from home at Valley Forge. On July 31, he recorded in his diary that he rode "over the old cantonment of the American army of the winter of 1777 and 1778; visited all the works, which were in ruins, and the encampments in woods where the grounds had not been cultivated." On that visit, the former commander in chief also stopped to have a conversation with a local farmer about how to cultivate buckwheat as food for cattle.

The convention finally opened on May 25. Of the seventy-four delegates named to the convention, fifty-five showed up. With an average age of forty-three (ranging from twenty-four to eighty-one), and representing twelve states, they were generally prosperous citizens who tended to be more moderate than either rigidly conservative or liberal in nature. They were lawyers, farmers, planters, and businessmen; twenty-one were veterans of the Revolutionary War; eight had signed the Declaration of Independence. The proceedings were also noteworthy for who was *not* in attendance. The state of Rhode Island, in protest, refused to participate—as did such individual delegates as Samuel Adams and Patrick Henry who vehe-

mently disapproved of the entire concept of a national constitution. Thomas Jefferson (whose wife had died) was in Paris,
having taken Franklin's place, and John Adams was still on
diplomatic duty in London.

The delegates met in the same room at the State House
where the Declaration of Independence had been signed in
1776. Almost immediately, the group decided to impose a gag
order on the proceedings. Armed sentries were placed outside
the doors so that no news leaked out—which tended to infu-
riate the numerous lobbyists who were worried that their own
special interests would in some way be harmed by the final
outcome of the convention. The reason for secrecy was simple. The delegates knew they were going to be making some
changes, perhaps big changes. And they did not want their debates influenced by outside parties.

After establishing some basic parliamentary rules, the convention then unanimously elected George Washington as its
chairman. Somewhat embarrassed, Washington lamented his
qualifications, but also expressed not only his commitment to
the proceedings, but also his faith in the American people.
"[I'm] sure the mass of citizens in the United States mean
well," he said, "and I firmly believe they will always act well
whenever they can obtain a right understanding of matters."
During the entire four months of proceedings, Washington
sat at the head of the delegation and moderated debate. And
knowing the value of silence, he interrupted the convention
only one time to speak his mind.

There were two overarching principles that all the delegates
held in common. First, they believed that only a government
that derived its authority and power from its citizens would
merit the sacrifice of those who served in the American Revolution. And second, the people should have a direct voice in
determining how their government was run and who should
run it.

Many of the delegates made eloquent statements during the
early going. George Mason of Virginia advocated that: "We

ought to attend to the rights of every class of the people [and] provide no less carefully for the happiness of the lowest than of the highest orders of citizens." John Dickinson of Connecticut said: "Let our government be like that of the solar system. Let the general government be like the sun and the states the planets, repelled yet attracted, and the whole moving regularly and harmoniously in their several orbits."

And, adroitly playing the part of the elder statesman emeritus, Benjamin Franklin counseled tolerance and forbearance to his fellow delegates. "We are sent here to *consult*, not to *contend* with each other," he said. "Positiveness and warmth on one side, naturally beget their like on the other; and tend to create and augment discord and division in a great concern, wherein harmony and union are extremely necessary to give weight to our councils, and render them effectual in promoting and securing the common good.

"This assembly," stated Franklin, "[is] groping in the dark, as it were, to find political truth."

James Madison, who strategically positioned himself in the first row close to George Washington's desk, told the delegation that "the eyes and hopes of all are turned toward this new assembly," and that "there can be no doubt that the result will in some way or other have a powerful effect on our [nation's] destiny." Actually, Madison was not only totally committed to a strong national constitution, he was the best-prepared delegate at the entire convention. He showed up in Philadelphia eleven days early and, because the other delegates straggled in, he ended up waiting around for nearly three weeks. However, Madison did not spend his time idly whiling away the hours. Rather he kept going over his plans, methodically, carefully—and then revising his strategy. And once the proceedings finally got going, his influence was so pronounced that Madison has often been called the "Chief Architect of the Constitution."

As a leader, Madison was smart, tenacious, and possessed a high dose of humility. "The better any man is," he said, "the lower thoughts he has of himself." He studied human nature and knew that people were more apt to pursue short-term rather than long-term interests. Moreover, Madison thought deeply about the elements of governance and political theory. All of these traits and talents helped him sway his colleagues at the convention. But his most enduring characteristic was that he was achievement-oriented. And, as such, he persistently and purposefully studied, planned, and prepared for what was to be the greatest achievement of his lifetime—the creation of a strong and effective national constitution for the United States.

Months before the start of the convention, Madison organized a series of meetings with the entire seven-man Virginia delegation. Together, they hammered out a preliminary blueprint that was to provide the basis for all future discussion of a new federal government. The Virginia plan proposed three separate branches of government—legislative, executive, and judicial—all equal in stature, each providing a check on the others.

More importantly, it was a completely new idea—a simple proposal that, when presented to the convention at large, caught all the other delegates by surprise. It was imaginative, creative, audacious, and almost radiant in its artistic balance and symmetry. The more the delegates thought about it, the more they liked it. Virginia's plan, largely the brainchild of James Madison, was adopted by the convention within the first two weeks. Accordingly, it became the foundation of all future democratic governments.

Most of the rest of the convention (nearly three and one half months) revolved around ironing out the specifics of how the three branches of government would be created and ultimately function. However, as the devil always seems to be in the details, the Constitutional Convention nearly fell apart during the fight over exactly how the legislature was to be proportioned. It was at this point that the ongoing sibling fight between the large and small states reared its ugly head.

The large states liked the idea of both a House of Representatives and a Senate that were comprised of members in direct proportion to the population of America. But the small states steadfastly maintained that both houses have equal representation for each state no matter what the population. Their idea was: "one state—one vote." And because of the bitter hatred and jealousy that had been festering for years, neither of the two factions was willing to budge an inch.

Finally, Roger Sherman, a delegate from Connecticut who had also signed the Declaration of Independence, suggested a compromise whereby the House of Representatives would be based on population and the Senate based on state equality. At first, few liked the idea and most were inclined to pass on it. But Benjamin Franklin chose to speak up at this critical moment—and when the distinguished elder statesman spoke, everyone else listened intently.

He urged the delegates to remember that the convention would fail if there was not mutual sacrifice among those in the room. And, as was his practice, Franklin used a metaphor to persuade his colleagues to budge a bit: "When a broad table is to be made, and the edges of the planks do not fit, the artist takes a little from both and makes a good joint," he said. "In like manner here, both sides must part with some of their demands, in order that they may join in some accommodating proposition." Shortly thereafter, the representatives, moved by the old man's eloquence, agreed to seek a compromise solution. Benjamin Franklin, although he said little, had broken the logjam and saved the convention.

When Sherman brought up his idea once again, a vote was called for and the result was an even split—five for, five against, one abstention, one not present. The majority of the delegates then agreed to leave the decision to a smaller committee comprised of one delegate from each state. Franklin was voted onto the committee, Madison was not. A few days later, in what has since been dubbed "The Great Compromise," this council made its report back to the general membership. They recommended the House be comprised of representatives based solely on population. The formula would be one delegate for every 40,000 people. The Senate, on the other hand, would be removed from direct popular control and be comprised of two members from each state.

Most of the delegates were pleased with the compromise solution. Several, however, refused to accept it. Two of the three delegates from New York, for example, left the convention in protest and declared they would not return (Alexander Hamilton stayed). Upon their departure, one representative who had served in the war observed that "the look on George Washington's face reminded me of its expression during the terrible months we were in Valley Forge camp."

But the convention managed to plow ahead and, with the spirit of compromise now in the air, the delegates found middle ground on the other divisive issue of the proceedings—slavery. In the end, they agreed to permit slave importation until 1808 after which time it would cease. They strategically decided not to make the Constitutional Convention a forum on the merits of slavery. They were there to create a new government. The slavery issue, though troubling and at odds with democratic political thought, would have to be settled sometime in the future by another generation. First things first.

The representatives then set up a Committee of Detail that was charged with organizing the material that had been discussed and approved. Edmund Randolph, one of the members, urged that only the most important overarching principles be included so that government processes would not be subjected to unalterable details. The rest of the committee was comprised of Nathaniel Gorham of Massachusetts, Oliver Ellsworth of Connecticut, John Rutledge of South Carolina, and James Wilson of Pennsylvania.

This group of five created a concise document well organized into articles and sections and presented it to the general convention on August 6. Nearly all of the delegates were pleased with the result. But with such a new perspective, additional thoughts and concerns were generated. As a result, another five weeks of debate ensued as every paragraph was discussed and voted upon. During that time, among other things, the representatives provided a process for adding amendments to the constitution and created a Supreme Court to resolve interpretations of the new framework.

After the Committee of Detail finished its work, still another five-man group was formed to "revise the style of and arrange the articles which had been agreed to by the House." The Committee of Style and Arrangement was manned by James Madison, Alexander Hamilton, William Samuel Johnson (Vermont), Rufus King (Massachusetts), and Gouverneur Morris (Pennsylvania).

One would logically assume that either Madison or Hamilton, because of their past work, would exert leadership of the group in order to place the final touches on the document. However, both stepped back and followed the lead of Morris, whose strengths included a creative and artistic literary skill. In turn, Morris advocated a document with grace and symmetry in addition to a concise structure. He wanted the constitution to be simply worded with plain, common language that everyone could clearly understand—but also with a certain amount of vagueness and flexibility.

So it was Gouverneur Morris, a relatively unknown American patriot, who personally—and perhaps appropriately—sat down and wrote out the opening paragraph to the new constitution. With grace and ease—as if it was meant to be, as if he was writing for all average citizens everywhere—the words flowed from his quill pen:

> We the people of the United States, in order to
> form a more perfect union, establish justice, insure
> domestic tranquillity, provide for the common de-
> fense, promote the general welfare, and secure the
> blessings of liberty to ourselves and our posterity,

do ordain and establish this Constitution for the United States of America.

This Preamble reflected the essence of the "national character" that George Washington had talked about establishing. The new constitution (and thereby the government and the culture that was about to be created) was to be the servant of the people rather than their king.

In thinking through and preparing the document, the founding fathers astutely applied their insight into human nature. They knew, for instance, that factions would exist; that some people would seek power for their own ends; that self-interest could be abusive when provided the opportunity; and that passion and emotion could often override reason.

They knew all this because they had seen it happen in the common system of administration in Great Britain where the monarchy was strongly attached to the Parliament. Such merging of the executive and legislative powers of government allowed oppressive legislation to pass while exempting those who passed it from its consequences and effects. Where a monarchy existed, the government was only as good as the individual in control at the moment. On the other hand, the founding fathers were also acutely aware that there could easily be a tyranny of the majority. A bad idea carried too far by too many people could easily become oppressive.

So they thought through the processes of government and combined that knowledge with their insight into the way people interacted and reacted to various situations. Essentially, they were dealing with 500 years of experiments that had proven ineffective. They pondered how to build a system so that the idealism contained in the Magna Carta could be employed in practical operation.

In this instance, the framers of the Constitution realized they had the unique opportunity to sit down and say to themselves: "How can we do this right; really right." And when it came down to it, they all seized upon that opportunity and agreed to depart from tradition to try something completely new and different. They created a system of government that attempted to embrace the natural goodness of humankind while, at the same time, guarding against the darker side of human nature.

The executive branch, for example, maintained the positive aspects of a single leadership authority, but removed the negative ones. The people would still have a president who could provide new ideas and attempt to inspire the masses; one person who could make executive decisions; one person who could stand in the way of the potential tyranny of the majority. On the other hand, the single executive could not become a tyrant because of the system of checks and balances in place. Therefore, one crazy idea coming from the ivory tower, could not make it through the entire system unless the majority of the people agreed.

These two arms of the legislative branch—combined with a strong, but power-limited executive—were intended to provide an effective system of social and governmental checks and balances (social in the House; governmental in the Senate). Theoretically, it would be extremely difficult to stack all three to obtain the self-serving ends of any particular group of dissidents. In essence, the system would force people to stop and think things through before acting. Any issue, once on the table, had to be discussed before passage and enactment. As a result, sponsors would have to go back and rethink, refine, and make their plans stronger. As James Madison was later to write in *The Federalist Papers*, the new government would "cure the mischief of factions."

Moreover, the Constitution created a culture that purposefully and intentionally forced both consensus-building and compromise. It encouraged a process of achievement where everyone came out ahead, where progress was made. This premise is well articulated in Stephen R. Covey's idea of the Win/Win situation. In *The Seven Habits of Highly Effective*

People, he described it as "a total philosophy of human inter-action":

> Win/Win is a frame of mind and heart that con-stantly seeks mutual benefit in all human interac-tions. [It] means that agreements or solutions are mutually beneficial, mutually satisfying. With a Win/Win solution, all parties feel good about the decision and feel committed to the action plan. Win/Win sees life as a cooperative, not a compet-itive arena. . . . It's based on the [idea] that there is plenty for everybody, that one person's success is not achieved at the expense or exclusion of the success of others.

In addition to creating a situation where everybody wins, skilled compromise can be a leader's key to success—especially in changing times when attempting to break new ground. Be-cause people are so resistant to change, it is often the only practical method that allows leaders to make any progress at all in achieving their goals. And since the definition of leader-ship omits the use of coercive power, compromise effectively becomes the tool of a true leader—one who attempts to move followers through persuasion and inspiration rather than co-ercion.

And while the new Constitution effectively encouraged compromise, it also fostered a classic creative process—by providing an avenue for fresh ideas to be spawned and then guaranteeing that they would be heard. The best thoughts, once popped into the system, would rise to the top; the worst would fall by the wayside. And because a diverse group had to approve of new ventures, it impelled people to apply them-selves; to have a dialogue with others; to search for common ground; to work in a team; to persuade and inspire. And fi-nally, through the free election of representatives, this would be a government that empowered the people by truly involving them. It was a system that mobilized citizens if they wanted to mobilize; to have a say if they wanted a say. In truth, then, the new Constitution of the United States facilitated nothing less than the art of leadership itself—and very creative leadership, at that. The chief executive (to be called a "president"), for instance, could not be a dictator. He would have a great deal of responsibility, but not all the authority. Therefore, he would have to persuade and inspire followers. He would have to be a true leader.

The Constitution of the United States of America created a new culture for a new nation. It established a character—of honesty, integrity, and human rights. It provided a standard of excellence for which to strive. And it created an understanding; an understanding that this organization—this United States of America—was a place where people would be free; free to practice the religion of their choice; free to think whatever was on their minds; and free to speak their thoughts.

Great leaders know that an organization possessing a strong culture will always win over one that does not. They realize that people will die for a cause, but not for a job; that winners attract winners; and that the best people will want to be a part of the best organizations. Every long-lasting enterprise, whether a nation or a business corporation, needs a well-thought-through culture; one with high ethical standards, vibrancy, energy, and openness; one where fairness and freedom are the norm.

The Constitution, which outlined the culture of the United States, was a work of collective genius by a group of people with different thoughts and beliefs who came together from different geographic regions of the country. When Thomas Paine read the document, he recognized that "a new era for politics [was] struck," and that "a new method of thinking [had] arisen." When described as *the* writer of the Constitution, Madison countered that "it ought to be regarded as the work of many heads and many hands." "It was done by bargain and compromise," said Nicholas Gilman, a delegate from document. Others signed with significant reservations. Alexander Hamilton, in defiance of political powers in his state, rode in from New York at the last second to place his name on the historic document—even though two thirds of his delegation had left in protest.

As the delegates signed, Benjamin Franklin pointed to a painting on the wall behind George Washington's desk. It depicted a sun low on the horizon. He casually mentioned that painters "often found it difficult to distinguish in their art a rising from a setting sun." Over the last four months, he had pondered the painting without being able to tell which it was. "But now at length," he whispered to those near him, "I have the happiness to know that it is a rising and not a setting sun."

When his turn came to sign, Benjamin Franklin wept.

After the signing ceremony had concluded, the delegates moved to entrust all official documents of the convention to George Washington "subject to the order of Congress, if ever formed under the Constitution."

"The business being closed," wrote Washington in his diary, "the members adjourned to the City Tavern, dined together and took a cordial leave of each other."

THE FOUNDING FATHERS ON LEADERSHIP

★ Form a culture that will give consistency, stability, and dignity to your organization.

★ Combine the past with the present to build a bridge to the future.

★ Turn an unsuccessful event into a clarion call for action.

★ When contemplating some big changes, keep out people with special interests. Include only those who want to do the right thing.

★ When forming a strategy team, *consult* rather than *contend* with each other.

★ Positiveness and warmth on one side naturally beget their like on the other.

★ In order to secure a major achievement, you must prepare in detail ahead of time.

★ The better any man is, the lower thoughts he has of himself.

★ Create small committees to resolve big issues.

★ Search for common ground and create a Win/Win situation. Remember that compromise is the tool of a true leader.

★ People will die for a cause, but not for a job.

★ Don't forget that winners attract winners.

★ Construct your culture with simplicity, flexibility, and elasticity so that it will be able to suffer hard knocks with little damage.

★ Always remain optimistic. See a rising sun rather than a setting sun.

"My hope was to gain time [for] our country to settle and mature . . . and to progress without interruption to that degree of strength and consistency which is necessary to give it, humanly speaking, the command of its own fortunes."

President George Washington,
Farewell Address,
March 4, 1797

"[We must] support every rational effort to encourage schools, colleges, universities, academies, and every institution for propagating knowledge, virtue, and religion among all people. [It is] the only means of preserving our constitution."

President John Adams,
Inaugural Address,
March 4, 1797

"This removes from us the greatest source of danger to our peace."

President Thomas Jefferson,
upon receiving word of the
official signing of the Louisiana
Purchase, July 3, 1803

"The advice nearest to my heart and deepest in my convictions is that the Union of the States be cherished and perpetuated."

President James Madison,
"Advice to My Country,"
October 1834

final battle of the Revolution. And America's great leaders once again rose to the occasion.

Almost instantly, Alexander Hamilton assumed the responsibility for seeing that a campaign of information and education reached the great majority of America's decision-makers. He created a series of newspaper articles called *The Federalist*, which appeared in newspapers under the pen name "Publius." Hamilton (who later came to be known as the "Ratifier of the Constitution") wrote fifty-one of the eighty-five *Federalist Papers*—and recruited James Madison to write twenty-nine, and John Jay (former president of the Continental Congress) to write five. *The Federalist* first appeared in October 1787—a month after the Constitutional Convention closed—and continued through May of 1788.

Hamilton, Madison, and Jay tried to think of every question the common citizen might have about the new Constitution—and then they came up with answers to those questions. Accordingly, Publius addressed issues of property, personal rights, and the tyranny of the majority. The authors also discussed how the Constitution essentially deregulated interstate commerce, how it guaranteed an environment friendly to private business, and how it encouraged economic growth. They also openly discussed their reasoning for proposing a three-tiered government that achieved equality and balance. "[It will be] less probable," wrote Madison in *Federalist No. 10*, "that a majority of the whole will have a common motive to invade the rights of other citizens; or if such a common motive exists, it will be more difficult for all who feel it to discover their own strength and to act in unison with each other."

Alexander Hamilton also read and listened intently to the arguments of those opposed to the Constitution. When a particular negative charge was made, Hamilton would dash off an immediate retort. In effect, Publius was able to equalize anything the Antifederalists said almost as fast as their

tions were held by each state in honor of the formation of a new government for their new and independent nation.

In early April of 1789, the first United States Congress convened in both the House of Representatives and Senate. Electors had previously (and unanimously) chosen George Washington as the new chief executive and John Adams his backup. When informed of his election on April 14, Washington hesitated. "I have no wish beyond that of living and dying an honest man on my own farm," he said. Still, he would not refuse his country's call.

In making preparations for his departure from Mount Vernon, Washington paid a visit to his ailing mother. It was the last time he would see her, as Mary Washington died only a few months later. And, because he had little cash on hand, he borrowed money from a friend to pay for his trip to New York, which was to be the first capital. Nevertheless, upon arriving, Washington offered to serve without salary. Congress, however, voted the position a $25,000 annual compensation package and, after wrestling for weeks about what the new chief executive should be called, the legislative branch finally decided on the title "President of the United States."

George Washington was inaugurated on April 30 at Federal Hall in New York City and, at James Madison's urging, made a short inaugural speech. "Integrity and firmness," he said, in part, "is all I can promise." The first president wore a brown velvet suit for the occasion—making sure to see that it was made in America.

In the fall of 1789, Congress established several new executive departments, including those of State, Treasury, and War. After consulting with a few key advisers (chief among them James Madison) the new president then set about building his team. He chose Thomas Jefferson to become the first secretary of state—and Alexander Hamilton for secretary of the treasury. Henry Knox, the former bookseller who had achieved the impossible at Dorchester Heights, was appointed secretary of war. Edmund Randolph of Virginia got the nod for the new office of attorney general. Washington also appointed a strong Supreme Court comprised of, among others, John Jay (as Chief Justice), John Rutledge of South Carolina, and James Wilson of Pennsylvania. Thomas Paine was eventually named the new president's personal envoy in London.

After undertaking a vigorous door-to-door campaign in his home district, James Madison got himself elected to the House of Representatives and became the new president's number one ally in Congress. And within a week of Washington's inauguration, Madison announced to the entire House that he intended to shortly introduce a Bill of Rights consisting of ten new amendments to the Constitution. He had not only heard the call of the people during the ratification process, but had also been heavily influenced to act by two of his friends and fellow Virginians, George Mason and Thomas Jefferson. Mason, the richest man in the state and author of both the Virginia constitution and the Virginia bill of rights, enthusiastically lobbied Madison and other congressmen for passage. And Jefferson, believing that inference alone was inadequate, passionately pushed for the specific mention of such individual liberties as freedom of the press and freedom of religion.

Accordingly, Madison drafted the first ten amendments to the Constitution and, through hard work and determination, managed to persuade the majority of his reluctant colleagues in Congress to approve them, in total, as one piece of legislation. Two and one half years later, on December 15, 1791, the Bill of Rights—which specifically guaranteed such individual rights as freedom of speech, religion, and so forth—was ratified by the states and became part of the Constitution.

The real creation of the Bill of Rights, however, did not come only from the pen of James Madison. Rather, it was the result of the process of ratification that followed the Constitutional Convention of 1787. The people at large, when pondering the new plan, requested that their individual rights be specifically enumerated. Madison, then, was acting as nothing more than a representative of the majority of American citizens—which is exactly what leaders are supposed to do.

The founding fathers essentially initiated action. They offered something new. They put an idea on the table, offered a fresh vision, and then asked followers for their input and support. They did not attempt to force the plan on the people. Rather, they attempted to persuade and inspire others of the merits of their proposal.

The Constitution of the United States was put together by representatives from the various states. The people clearly could have rejected the document outright. They did not, however, choose to do so. Rather, they accepted it as it was and then asked that something of their own be added later in order to make it not only better, but more reflective of their wishes. In other words, the people wanted their collective signature placed on the new Constitution.

As the first president, George Washington had to set the tone for all future presidents—as well as the direction for the new nation. Accordingly, he quickly turned to Adams, Jefferson, Hamilton, and Madison for advice on how to conduct himself in day-to-day matters of personal interaction. He decided to strike a balance between "too free an intercourse and too much familiarity." At first he saw anyone who would call on him but, because his day became so clogged with visitors, he changed his mind and limited visiting hours.

Washington also set precedents for presidential interaction with Congress. In matters of foreign affairs, he decided to take action first and then ask for the "advice and consent" of the Senate. When France declared war on Great Britain, for instance, and the Netherlands in 1793, President Washington declared America's neutrality in the conflict—and Congress did not object.

In 1794, when an excise tax on whiskey championed by Treasury Secretary Alexander Hamilton was enacted, tax collectors in western Pennsylvania were tarred and feathered as local farmers armed themselves and declared they would not pay. President Washington, alarmed at such a blatant rejection of federal authority, called out 13,000 militiamen and personally supervised their organization in the field. The army received virtually no opposition as it marched through several counties in Pennsylvania and arrested more than 150 people. Two men were eventually tried, convicted of treason, and sentenced to death. President Washington, however, pardoned both men—and the Whiskey Rebellion was put down. There would be very few challenges to federal authority in the wake of such tough action by the new chief executive.

During the course of his presidency, Washington also did such natural things as take Thomas Jefferson and Alexander Hamilton on a three-day fishing expedition in an attempt to get to know them better and help them settle their differences. He also got out of the ivory tower on a regular basis to keep in touch with the people, visiting New England and states of other regions on a frequent basis.

In all, George Washington served two terms as president. However, in another precedent-setting move, he declined to run for a third term preferring, rather, to "pass the torch" and return home to Mount Vernon. In his farewell address to the nation, Washington managed to communicate why he had agreed to serve as president in the first place. His hope, as he said, was "to gain time [for] our country to settle and mature . . . and to progress without interruption to that degree of strength and consistency which is necessary to give it, humanly speaking, the command of its own fortunes."

The new government survived the transfer of power from

one chief executive to another when John Adams succeeded Washington as the second president of the United States on March 4, 1797. In his inaugural address, Adams advocated the support of "every rational effort to encourage schools, colleges, universities, academies, and every institution for propagating knowledge, virtue, and religion among all people. [It is] the only means of preserving our constitution," he said. During his four years in office, Adams opened the Library of Congress, created the Department of the Navy, oversaw the eventual site of the new nation's capital, and became the first president to occupy the White House. He also had the distinction of appointing John Marshall, a veteran of Valley Forge, to the United States Supreme Court. And when the possibility of war again reared its head—this time with France—President Adams appointed a willing and able George Washington to be commander of the army. However, the former leader did not have to leave Mount Vernon, as the war never materialized.

Within the first decade after the ratification of the Constitution, a two-party system emerged as the dominant political culture of the new nation. The Federalist Party was led by Washington, Adams, and Hamilton, and the brand-new Democratic Party was founded by Jefferson and Madison. In November 1800, John Adams was defeated in his bid for reelection by Thomas Jefferson, who eked out a narrow victory over Aaron Burr when the contest was thrown into the House of Representatives. This peaceful transfer of executive power from one party to another served as a milestone for the new democratic system of government.

During his first term, President Jefferson seized upon an offer from Napoleon to purchase France's Louisiana Territory for $15 million. That figure translated into three cents an acre and effectively doubled the size of the United States by adding all or part of fifteen future states: Arkansas, Colorado, Iowa, Kansas, Louisiana, Minnesota, Missouri, Montana, Nebraska, New Mexico, North Dakota, Oklahoma,

South Dakota, Texas, and Wyoming. Jefferson closed the deal without consulting Congress and, when learning that France had signed the contract, said: "This removes from us the greatest source of danger to our peace."

Toward the end of his second term, Jefferson responded to an ill-fated conspiracy led by his former vice president, Aaron Burr, to instigate a war with Spain and seize lands acquired by the Louisiana Purchase. Burr was eventually captured in Mississippi, skipped out on his bond, was recaptured, tried for treason, and finally acquitted. The Jefferson administration, however, had acted quickly and decisively to quell yet another mini-rebellion in the wake of independence—this one coming a full decade after the signing of the Constitution and more than fifteen years after the war had ended.

As president, Jefferson frequently invited Thomas Paine over to the White House. Contemporaries noted that the two men enjoyed each other's company, always spoke to each other as equals, and could be seen frequently walking the White House grounds arm in arm.

James Madison, another close associate of President Jefferson's, served as his secretary of state for eight years, and then won election to the presidency himself in 1808. Madison led America during the War of 1812 (which is often called the "Second War of Independence" because it ended, once and for all, the nation's economic dependence on Great Britain). The war, which was fought over rights in international waters, once again united the individual states in a common cause. In essence, those old patriotic feelings of 1776 erupted and nearly every American chipped in to help.

Captain Oliver Hazard Perry took control of Lake Erie after a difficult three-hour naval battle. "We have met the enemy and they are ours," he wrote in a famous dispatch to his superiors. In August 1814, redcoats landed in the Chesapeake Bay and marched to Washington where they forced

President Madison and his wife to flee into neighboring Virginia. Dolley Madison, waiting until the last possible minute to leave, composed a letter to her sister that said, in part: "Two messengers covered with dust come to bid me fly; but . . . I insist on waiting until the large picture of George Washington is secured." The president and first lady returned three days later to find that the British had burned much of Washington, including the White House and the Capitol. One month later, at Fort McHenry in Baltimore, the American refusal to surrender during a fierce artillery bombardment inspired Francis Scott Key to write "The Star Spangled Banner"—later to become the national anthem of the United States.

Moreover, the future sixth, seventh, and ninth presidents of the United States figured heavily in the War of 1812. John Quincy Adams was America's chief negotiator at the Treaty of Ghent officially ending the war. General Andrew Jackson, assisted by the Marquis de Lafayette, who had once again jumped to America's defense, won a monumental defensive victory at New Orleans by repelling the British and losing only twenty-one men (as opposed to more than 2,000 British casualties). And William Henry Harrison fought valiantly in Kentucky, Ohio, and Canada after being commissioned a brigadier general.

As it was, James Madison (in 1816) passed the torch to his own secretary of state, James Monroe, who at the age of eighteen had been one of the four American soldiers wounded at the battle of Trenton. Monroe served two terms as president and is most famous for enacting the Monroe Doctrine, which proved to be an enduring cornerstone of American foreign policy. Basically, James Monroe served notice to the world that "the American continents [were] not to be considered as subjects for future colonization by any European powers."

*   *   *

Among people who wish to be leaders, but are unable to succeed, there exists a tendency to back off after a significant event has been accomplished. Statements often heard in such cases include: "Well, now that I've worked hard for three months, I think I'll lie back and catch up on my reading"; or "I've done my job, let somebody else do something for a change"; or "It's not my fault if we don't succeed, I did what I was supposed to do."

However, successful leaders never sit back and rest on their laurels. Washington, Adams, Jefferson, and Madison possessed a slow and steady fire of persistence, determination, and action. It is a proven maxim of leadership that the fire of a truly great leader is always burning.

The history books clearly demonstrate that America's founding fathers stuck around and followed through on what they had started. They did not rely on others to ensure success for future generations. They took it upon themselves to protect and fortify the foundation of democracy.

When mini-rebellions threatened to disrupt the new government, they were there to subdue the danger. When important principles needed to be strengthened, they were on hand to take care of it. And when the dark side of human nature flared up, they were there to douse the flames. In short, when their country called, the founding fathers came running—every single time.

The first forty-four years of the new nation's existence—from the signing of the Declaration of Independence to the end of Monroe's second term—were led by leaders directly involved in the American Revolution. Moreover, the founding fathers strategically developed future leaders and successfully passed the torch of liberty to the next generation. For it was none other than John Adams's son, John Quincy Adams, who succeeded James Monroe as the sixth president of the United States.

The feelings of the founding fathers regarding follow-through can be summed up in something James Madison wrote in October of 1834 (shortly before his death). A document entitled "Advice to My Country," released after he died, contained this simple sentence: "The advice nearest to my heart and deepest in my convictions is that the Union of the States be cherished and perpetuated."

THE FOUNDING FATHERS ON LEADERSHIP

★ Remember that initial reaction to significant change often involves outrage bordering on hysteria.

★ When introducing radical change, be prepared to be attacked personally—both verbally and physically.

★ It is in the nature of people to pursue their own interests.

★ Think of every possible question that might arise in opposition to your plan—and then come up with answers to those questions.

★ Counter scare tactics from the opposition by immediately refuting false charges.

★ Seize the initiative to educate people through the mass communication methods of the day.

★ Consult with trusted advisers prior to making appointments or establishing precedents.

★ Leaders act as agents of change for the majority of people they represent.

★ In order to get to know them better, take your top executives on a fishing expedition—or some similar enjoyable trip.

★ Successful leaders do not sit back and rest on their laurels.

★ The fire of a truly great leader is always burning.

★ Develop future leaders. Pass the torch to the next generation.

Epilogue

On July 4, 1994—218 years after the signing of the Declaration of Independence—Václav Havel, president of the Czech Republic, received America's Liberty Medal at Independence Hall in Philadelphia. In his acceptance speech, Havel noted the changing times: "Today, many things indicate that we are going through a transitional period, when it seems that something is on the way out and something else is painfully being born." People, he said, were searching "for new scientific recipes, new idealogies, new control systems, new institutions, new instruments" to replace those that no longer work. Havel also noted that there have been other periods in history "when values undergo a fundamental shift"— "when cultures distant in time and space are discovered or rediscovered. . . . In such an era," said Havel, "anything is possible."

The period surrounding the American Revolution was just such an era—a period of transition when tyranny was on the way out and democracy was painfully being born; when people searched for new idealogies; and when a new culture, never before attained, yet near to the heart of every human being, was finally conceived.

During this turbulent time in history, America's founding fathers, individually and collectively, stepped forward to lead the way. They did so, in part, because they realized that from profound change spring new opportunities—and this was a time where there would be a chance for them to make something happen.

They also stepped forward because they cared. They cared about the future generations who would follow. "I must study politics and war," wrote John Adams to his wife, Abigail, "so that my sons may have liberty to study mathematics and philosophy, geography [and] natural history . . . in order to give their children a right to study painting, poetry, [and] music. . . ."

America's leaders, and the people they led, then fought a Revolutionary War where, in the beginning, success seemed nothing more than a distant dream. But they tried anyway—persevering in the face of adversity; enduring almost unimaginable hardships and personal sacrifices. "It will not be believed," said George Washington after the war, "that such a force as Great Britain has employed for eight years in this country could be baffled in their plans . . . by men oftentimes half-starved, always in rage, without pay, and experiencing at times, every distress which human nature is capable of undergoing."

In 1776, those who signed the Declaration of Independence mutually pledged "their lives, their fortunes, and their sacred honor." Some were captured, tortured, and killed by the enemy. Some were thrown into prison. Others saw their families scattered, their homes burned, or their businesses bankrupted. None, however, lost their sacred honor. That was preserved by the generations who today live in a free society—all around the globe.

In the end, several of the founding fathers passed away while still in their forties. Nathanael Greene and John Paul Jones, both bankrupt and broken, died several years after the war ended. Alexander Hamilton was killed in a duel with Aaron Burr in 1804. Sam Adams, Patrick Henry, Paul Revere,

Robert Morris, and James Madison, however, lived long lives as respected elder statesmen and died of old age.

Thomas Paine, who had donated all his manuscript royalties to the cause, suffered from unemployment and depression for much of the rest of his life. He died of a stroke in 1806 at the age of seventy-two. Paine's body was lost, but his writings serve as his memorial.

Benjamin Franklin died peacefully in his sleep on April 17, 1790, at the age of eighty-four. His doctor said the end might have been brought on by "his love of fresh air, sitting at an open window for some hours with the cold air blowing in." Thomas Jefferson visited Franklin a few days before his death. "I found him in bed where he remains almost constantly," said Jefferson. "He had been clear of pain for some days and was cheerful and in good spirits."

On December 14, 1799, at age sixty-seven, George Washington—who had become known as the "Father of His Country"—passed away at Mount Vernon. Two days before, on a long ride around his plantation, he had been caught in a surprise winter storm of rain and snow. This would be the only storm he ever encountered that would get the best of him. The next day, he complained of a sore throat, grew hoarse, and then came down with severe chills and had extreme difficulty breathing. Washington was taking his own pulse when he died—and one of the last things he said was: "I am not afraid to go."

After their presidencies, John Adams retired to Braintree and Thomas Jefferson to Monticello. In later years, the two former political rivals carried on a long correspondence of letters that revealed much of their inner feelings and thoughts. Both men died peacefully on July 4, 1826—the fiftieth anniversary of the signing of the Declaration of Independence. Jefferson's last words were: "Is it the fourth?" Adams, who died a few hours later, said: "Jefferson lives."

During the American Revolution, America's founding fathers won an impossible victory by taking advantage of confusion, desperation, and urgency—and by practicing true leadership in the face of overwhelming adversity. Because they understood human nature, they knew that major change is more evolution than revolution; that tyranny and dictatorship are contradictory to the rights of the individual; and that leadership, in and of itself, is actually *in harmony* with human nature.

The founding fathers took a noble idea—one that their ancestors had dreamed about since the dawn of time—and then they did something about it. The great idea was that humankind had an inalienable right to be free. These men fought for that idea. And when they won their revolution, they tied the principles of humanity to a new and better system of government. The Declaration of Independence outlined those principles—and the Constitution of the United States created a culture that nurtured, cared for, and enhanced that new system, a system called democracy. The new three-part government structure was carefully crafted with checks and balances so that no one person, nor one faction, could oppress or terrorize the great majority of citizens.

Clearly, the founding fathers cleverly and shrewdly designed democracy to foster the art and process of leadership. And, in the final analysis, the principles of leadership are nothing less than the principles of humanity: treating people with respect and dignity; raising awareness; creating a vision and involving others; bonding together through alliances and teamwork; risking all; learning from mistakes; refusing to lose; inspiring rather than coercing; listening; compromising; caring; ever changing and ever achieving.

By practicing leadership themselves, and by instilling it in future generations, the founding fathers ensured, as Abraham Lincoln would later say, that "government of the people, by the people, for the people shall not perish from the earth."

In the spring of 1796, a farmer named Woodman was plowing his field at Valley Forge when he looked up and noticed a tall, distinguished-looking man standing silently with his hands behind his back.

It was George Washington—who had stopped by on his way home to Mount Vernon for the last time.

Woodman, himself a veteran of the Continental Army that had endured the harsh winter at Valley Forge, walked up the hill to greet his former leader. There, for the next several minutes, stood the farmer and the former president—having an amiable conversation about who knows what. Conceivably, they talked of agriculture or politics; or of what happened where they stood twenty years earlier. Maybe they even spoke of the future—of what they had left behind for future generations, for their posterity.

And perhaps Mr. Washington mentioned to Mr. Woodman something he had said not long after the end of the American Revolution:

> "If the people are not completely free and happy—the fault will be entirely their own."

"I have sworn, upon the altar of God, eternal hostility against every form of tyranny over the mind of man."

Thomas Jefferson,
November 23, 1800

Bibliography

Bailyn, Bernard. *Faces of Revolution: Personalities and Themes in the Struggle for American Independence.* New York: Vintage, 1992.

Banning, Lance. *Jefferson and Madison: Three Conversations from the Founding.* Madison: Madison House, 1995.

————.*The Sacred Fire of Liberty: James Madison and the Founding of the Federal Republic.* Ithaca: Cornell University Press, 1995.

Bennis, Warren, and Burt Nanus. *Leaders.* New York: Perennial Library, Harper & Row, 1985.

Bowen, Catherine Drinker. *Miracle at Philadelphia: The Story of the Constitutional Convention, May to September 1787.* Boston: Little, Brown, 1966.

Bradford, M. E. *Founding Fathers: Brief Lives of the Framers of the United States Constitution.* Lawrence: University Press of Kansas, 1994.

Brant, Irving. *James Madison: Father of the Constitution, 1787–1800.* New York: Bobbs-Merrill, 1950.

Brinker, Norman, and Donald T. Phillips. *On the Brink: The Life and Leadership of Norman Brinker.* Arlington, Texas: Summit, 1996.

Brookhiser, Richard. *Founding Father: Rediscovering George Washington.* New York: The Free Press, 1996.

Burns, James McGregor. *Leadership*. New York: Harper Torchbooks, 1978.

Callahan, North. *George Washington: Soldier and Man*. New York: William Morrow, 1972.

Clark, Ronald W. *Benjamin Franklin: A Biography*. New York: Da Capo Press, 1983.

Commager, Henry Steele, and Richard B. Morris, editors. *The Spirit of Seventy-Six: The Story of the American Revolution as Told by Participants*. New York: Da Capo Press, 1995.

Covey, Stephen R. *Principle-Centered Leadership*. New York: Simon and Schuster, 1990.

———. *The Seven Habits of Highly Effective People*. New York: Simon and Schuster, 1989.

DeGregorio, William A. *The Complete Book of U.S. Presidents*. New York: Dembner Books, 1984.

Fischer, David Hackett. *Paul Revere's Ride*. New York: Oxford University Press, 1994.

Flexner, James Thomas. Washington: *The Indispensable Man*. Boston: Little, Brown, 1969.

Forbes, Esther. *Paul Revere and the World He Lived In*. New York: Book-of-the-Month Club, 1983.

Franklin, Benjamin. *Writings*. New York: The Library of America, 1987.

Gardner, Howard. *Creating Minds*. New York: Basic Books, 1993.

———. *Leading Minds*. New York: Basic Books, 1995.

Grafton, John. *The American Revolution: A Picture Sourcebook*. New York: Dover, 1975.

Hamilton, Alexander, James Madison, and John Jay. *The Federalist Papers*. New York: Bantam, 1982.

Kaminski, John P., and Jill Adair McCaughan. *A Great and Good Man: George Washington in the Eyes of His Contemporaries*. Madison: Madison House, 1989.

Katzenbach, Jon R., and Douglas K. Smith. *The Wisdom of Teams*. Boston: Harvard Business School Press, 1993.

Keane, John. *Tom Paine*. Boston: Little, Brown, 1995.

Ketchum, Richard M. *The American Heritage Book of the Revolution.* New York: American Heritage, 1958.

Jackson, John W. *Valley Forge: Pinnacle of Courage.* Gettysburg: Thomas Publications, 1992.

Langguth, A. J. *Patriots: The Men Who Started the American Revolution.* New York: Simon and Schuster, 1988.

Leckie, Robert. *George Washington's War: The Saga of the American Revolution.* New York: HarperPerennial, 1992.

Madison, James. *Notes of Debates in the Federal Convention of 1787.* New York: W. W. Norton, 1987.

Malone, Dumas. *Jefferson, the Virginian.* Boston: Little Brown, 1948.

Mayer, Henry. *A Son of Thunder.* Charlottesville: University Press of Virginia, 1991.

McCullough, David. *Truman.* New York: Simon and Schuster, 1992.

McDonald, Forrest. *The Presidency of George Washington.* Lawrence, Kansas: University Press of Kansas, 1974.

McPhee, John. *Assembling California.* New York: Farrar, Straus & Giroux, 1993.

Middlekauff, Robert. *The Glorious Cause: The American Revolution, 1763–1789.* New York: Oxford University Press, 1982.

Mount Vernon Ladies Association. *George Washington's Rules of Civility and Decent Behaviour in Company and Conversation.* Mount Vernon, Virginia, 1989.

———. *Maxims of George Washington.* Mount Vernon, Virginia, 1989.

Paine, Thomas. *Collected Writings.* New York: The Library of America, 1995.

Peters, Tom, and Robert J. Waterman. *In Search of Excellence.* New York: Harper & Row, 1982.

Peters, Tom, and Nancy Austin. *A Passion for Excellence.* New York: Random House, 1985.

Peterson, Merrill D. *The Portable Thomas Jefferson.* New York: The Viking Press, 1975.

Phillips, Donald T. *Lincoln on Leadership*. New York: Warner Books, 1992.

Purcell, Edward L., and David F. Burg, editors. *The World Almanac of the American Revolution*. New York: World Almanac, 1992.

Ramsay, David, M.D. *The History of the American Revolution*. Indianapolis: Liberty Fund, 1990.

Senge, Peter. *The Fifth Discipline*. New York: Currency/ Doubleday, 1990.

Smith, Page. *John Adams*. New York: Doubleday, 1962.

Stokesbury, James L. *A Short History of the American Revolution*. New York: Quill/William Morrow, 1991.

Thane, Elswyth. *The Fighting Quaker: Nathanael Greene*. New York: Hawthorne, 1972.

Twain, Mark. *Life on the Mississippi*. Harper's Magazine, 1863.

Van Doren, Carl. *Benjamin Franklin*. New York: Penguin, 1991.

Acknowledgments

I'd like to acknowledge the foresight and good will of Larry Kirshbaum at Warner Books for suggesting this book and making it a reality. Bob Barnett, the best legal mind and literary agent in the business, was instrumental in bringing the work to publication. And Rick Wolff, a great editor at Warner, contributed significantly to the content and organization of the manuscript.

Karen Harrington, Norman Brinker, and Roger Sanders provided encouragement and insight throughout the process.

I'd also like to thank my parents, Alice and Don Phillips, for their support, comment, and feedback; and my wife, Susan, and children, Steve, Dave, and Kate, for everything.

DTP
Fairview, Texas

Index